PONY CLUB MANUAL
NUMBER ONE

This is the first of three manuals commissioned by the Pony Clubs Association for the guidance of children, young people and new riders taking up riding from the beginning. It is also essential reading for parents who wish to understand what their children (and they themselves) are embarking upon.

Manual One gives the basics for the beginner, taking him wisely and with understanding through all the subjects required, up to the standards for qualification for the Pony Club D and C Certificates.

These include, after useful preliminary Notes for Parents: the choice of pony and paddock; riding; jumping; competitions; the care of the pony — diet, exercise, grooming, shoeing and health; and saddlery and equipment.

The authors were chosen by the Pony Clubs Association for their extensive and successful experience of teaching riders and instructors, and their skills as author-photographers. Their work has the approval of instructor-colleagues and horse-specialist veterinarians. The resulting text is simple, lucid and comprehensive.

Action photographs and beautifully clear line drawings complete a pony club textbook and riding manual that is a model of its kind.

Manual Two is for more advanced riders, and *Manual Three* is for Pony Club instructors.

D0108939

Books by Elaine Knox-Thompson
and Suzanne Dickens

Guide to Riding and Horse Care (Lansdowne 1977,
1979, 1984, 1988: Orbis UK 1981, Merehurst UK 1985,
Howell US 1985)

The Young Horse (Collins 1979, 1985)

Horses and Ponies (Shortland 1989)

Pony Club Manual No. 1 (1981, 1982, 1984, 1986, 1988, 1990, 1991)

Pony Club Manual No. 2 (1985, 1988, 1990)

Pony Club Manual No. 3: For Instructors (1989, 1991)

The three *Manuals* are published by
Ray Richards Publisher
in conjunction with the
New Zealand Pony Clubs Association Inc.

Horse Sense (TVNZ 1982)
Television Series by Elaine Knox-Thompson
and Suzanne Dickens

PONY CLUB MANUAL
Number One

by

Elaine Knox-Thompson
BHSI, IIH

and Suzanne Dickens
BHSI, IIH

Drawings by Megan Harvey
Photographs by Suzanne Dickens

Auckland
RAY RICHARDS PUBLISHER

First published 1981
Reprinted 1982, 1984, 1986, 1988, 1990, 1991
RAY RICHARDS PUBLISHER
49 Aberdeen Road, Auckland 9
in conjunction with
New Zealand Pony Clubs Association

ISBN 0-908596-12-X

Designed by Don Sinclair
Typeset by Linotype Service (PN) Limited
Printed by Colorcraft Limited

CONTENTS

Foreword by Roland R. Matthews 6

Introduction 7

Acknowledgments 10

1. Notes for Parents 11

PART ONE — D CERTIFICATE (Test sheet) 19

2. Riding: D Certificate 20

3. Care of the Pony: D Certificate 35

PART TWO — C CERTIFICATE (Test sheet) 42

4. Riding: C Certificate 45

5. Out and About with Your Pony (C) 65

6. Jumping (C) 79

7. Competitions 94

8. Problem Ponies 112

PART THREE — CARE OF THE PONY 121

9. Paddocking: C Certificate 122

10. Watering, Feeding and Exercise (C) 128

11. Handling, Grooming, Shoeing,
    Measurements, Colours and Markings (C) 141

12. Health, Ailments and Injuries (C) 158

PART FOUR — SADDLERY AND EQUIPMENT 173

13. What You Need and How to Use It (C) 175

INDEX 199

FOREWORD

Ten years have elapsed since the *Pony Club Manual No. 1* was published in 1981. In excess of 36,000 copies have been published for young riding enthusiasts in New Zealand, and now Pony Club groups in Australia, Canada, U.S.A., South Africa and England are recognising the importance of this quick-to-learn book for their young riders. This is not an unexpected response when one realises that the authors Elaine Knox-Thompson and Suzanne Dickens have devoted a life-time to sharing their wealth of professional knowledge and experience with the Pony Club movement in England, New Zealand and Australia.

This first riding manual deals with all essential matters, from the purchase of a first pony to competing with that pony, and ensuring the real enjoyment to be found in the riding and owning of a pony. It covers the care of the pony, its feeding and health, and advice to parents for the improvement of their knowledge.

It is a fine publication and essential reading for all young riders, to help them systematically to progress with horsemastership and riding skills for the attainment of their D and C Certificates. The true success of this manual is clearly reflected in the greater depth of knowledge and abilities being achieved by our younger riders as they pass through the Certificate levels and on to completing the highest attainments in Pony Club, the H and A Certificates.

Since the publication of this manual Elaine Knox-Thompson and Suzanne Dickens have published *Manual No. 2* for C+, B, A and H attainments and *Manual No. 3* for Instructors.

These give the Pony Clubs Associations a complete and comprehensive set of three manuals unequalled by any other equestrian series. Our thanks and congratulations go to the authors for their outstanding achievements.

ROLAND R. MATTHEWS
President N.Z. Pony Clubs Assn

INTRODUCTION

PONY CLUB — WHAT IT'S ALL ABOUT

PONY CLUB started in England in 1928. It is a youth club for everybody interested in riding and horses, and it is now the biggest organisation of riders in the world.

The New Zealand Pony Clubs Association was founded by the late Mrs Dorothy Campbell in 1946. Its membership is now one of the highest, in proportion to the population, in the world. There are over eighty clubs, many of them with several branches, so wherever you live in New Zealand, you can be sure that there is a Pony Club not far away.

The objects of the New Zealand Pony Clubs Association are set out below. Numbers 3, 4 and 5 are the ones that will probably interest you most at present.

OBJECTS OF THE NEW ZEALAND PONY CLUBS ASSOCIATION

1. To encourage the formation of Pony Clubs in New Zealand and to regulate the general line of instruction in horsemanship and horse-mastership.
2. To subscribe to, become a member of, affiliate with, cooperate with and give donations and assistance to any other organisation or institution having aims and objects similar to those of the Association.
3. To encourage young people to ride and enjoy all kinds of sport connected with horses and riding, to instil in them the proper care of their animals, and to offer them the opportunity of receiving instruction of a higher class and on more orthodox lines than many of them can obtain individually.
4. To promote and conduct rallies, gymkhanas, competitions and hunter trials for young people.
5. To promote the highest ideals of sportsmanship, citizenship and loyalty, thereby cultivating strength of character and self-discipline.

Whatever your ambition, whether it be the faraway thought of riding for your country overseas, or simply to own and ride a pony for the sheer pleasure of it, Pony Club has much to offer: instruction — games — treks — companionship — competitions — all these are part of Pony Club life.

What you make of it is largely up to you. However young you are, your interest and sportsmanship will play a big part in the success of the whole club. If you attend regularly and take part in all possible activities, it will be rewarding to you and to your instructors. These people give a tremendous amount of time and effort to ensure that rallies are as interesting and helpful as possible — your attendance and enjoyment make it all worthwhile. Make sure you know the names at least of your own instructor and the head instructor, and always remember to thank them at the end of each rally. Tell them when you have specially enjoyed something — otherwise they may not know!

Whatever your mount, equipment, interest, standard — you will be welcome at Pony Club.

This is the basic manual, written for all those, whatever their age, who are starting in Pony Club. It covers riding and care of the pony up to C Certificate level. Since so many riders are keen to compete, it also includes guidance for preparation and training, to help you to get started in a variety of events.

The work is divided into Certificates to make it absolutely clear what is expected of you at each level. For instance, if you have learnt all that is contained in the D section, Riding and Pony Care, and can carry it out, then that is *all* you could expect to be asked for D Certificate.

While there is no compulsion, it is hoped that you will do your best to attain C Certificate. The C Test Sheet may look alarming at first glance, but it should not be beyond any member who has read this book thoroughly, has attended Pony Club regularly and has made an effort to form good habits in riding and pony care from the beginning.

Although the syllabus is wide, a really deep knowledge of any subject is not expected at this stage. The main objectives are to ensure that everybody can ride well enough to establish a safe and happy partnership with their pony, and that all ponies are cared for to a reasonable standard. Surely any pony owner will be eager to attain at least this level of knowledge and efficiency?

This *Manual* is not intended to go beyond the basics of Pony Club activities. When you have absorbed this one, you should read the *Pony Club Manual No. 2*, which covers the following things:

More advanced riding and jumping, including area trials and championships.

Preparation for dressage tests.

Training a young horse, including lungeing.

Looking after a stabled hore.

All necessary information for C+, B, A and H Certificates.

In fact, everything the older members need to know as they go through Pony Club.

Pony Club would be the first to agree that there are often several different methods of doing the same things, and that all the methods will achieve results. But, to avoid confusion, we believe it is essential to have clear guidelines for everyone to work on. The methods laid down here are all well tried — worldwide — and have been proved to be safe and to work for the majority of Pony Club members. All Certificates are based on these two manuals.

ACKNOWLEDGMENTS

We express our thanks and appreciation to the New Zealand Pony Clubs Association for the honour they paid us in inviting us to produce the official manuals of the Association, and for their patience and forbearance during the three long years that this first manual has been in the making.

We thank also the National Instructors of the New Zealand Pony Clubs Association, all of whom hold the qualification of British Horse Society Instructor (BHSI). They have been our advisory panel in checking the suitability of this manual for young riders and have given much time and care to reading and commenting on our manuscript. This included much discussion, some compromise and finally complete agreement. We acknowledge here the gratitude we have to our instructor colleagues: Suzanne Bason, Janey Fisher, Margaret Harris, Cheryl Monds, and Jenny Young.

The Training Committee of the New Zealand Pony Clubs Association, themselves instructors of many years experience, also gave much time to reading and commenting on the manuscript.

We are sure that all will share our appreciation of Megan Harvey's clear and accurate drawings and diagrams. Her skill and patience were boundless.

Six unnamed 'guinea-pigs', ordinary Pony Club members, spent hours of tedious repetition and enabled us to get exactly the photographs we needed. We congratulate them on the turnout of themselves and their splendid ponies — just the sensible, all-round types we seek for our D and C Certificate riders.

A few Pony Club instructors — alas, too few — made suggestions for this manual. They will doubtless recognise the passages that incorporate their thoughts.

Jennifer Stobart, the New Zealand Horse Society National Instructor, read the manuscript and made constructive suggestions.

John Noble, BVSc, and Peter Marshall, BVSc, both veterinarians of wide experience in the horse world, read, suggested amendments to, and finally approved the 'Health' chapter.

Taupo District Pony Club freely granted us the use of their excellent grounds and facilities.

The Sportsmen's Den, Taupo, generously loaned saddlery for the pictures in Part IV.

Finally, our appreciation to the publishing team of Ray Richards, Arnold Wall and Don Sinclair. We are extremely lucky to have such a fund of expertise. Their sympathy and assistance with the intricacies involved in a manual such as this have been encouraging throughout.

E.K-T. and S.D.

1
NOTES FOR PARENTS

PARENTS WHO RIDE, particularly those who have been through Pony Club themselves, will already know what having a pony in the family entails. So these notes are written mainly to assist parents who have never ridden, or possibly have little knowledge of animals of any kind.

If you are in the latter category, we strongly recommend that, *before* buying a pony, you should contact your local Pony Club. They will give you a good idea of what is involved financially in your district, and will also give help and advice in the basic essentials of finding a paddock and buying the pony and equipment.

ADVANTAGES OF RIDING

Riding is not a cheap sport, but its benefits are enormous. It provides healthy outdoor exercise; it can be enjoyed alone or in company, and this enjoyment can continue thoughout one's life. It also provides occupation. By the time the child has caught, groomed, ridden and fed the pony — not to mention cleaning the tack and chatting with other pony owners — there is neither time nor inclination for loitering about on street corners. With proper parental support and assistance, riding can do a very great deal to develop responsibility, understanding, and sportsmanship in the young.

RESPONSIBILITIES

Your child's first pony will certainly entail many new responsibilities for you. The pony really is a member of the family, and if it has to live several kilometres away, this will add to your problems.

Please read 'Paddocking   C Certificate ' (page 122) carefully, so that you will know just what is involved. If you have suitable land of your own or can arrange grazing at Pony Club, where help and advice are available, this will be much easier. But paddocks are usually hard to find in town areas — those small empty sections that look so tempting at first glance are not often suitable for ponies, and many ponies suffer considerably when forced to live in them. Check once again the 'Requirements of a Pony at Grass', on page 122, and 'What To Look For When Choosing A Paddock', on page 122. Whatever happens, proper grazing must be arranged *before* buying the pony.

WHERE TO RIDE?

A question often overlooked in town areas. Busy city streets are dangerous for young riders and their ponies, besides being very little fun once the initial novelty has worn off. Riding in the pony's own paddock also palls before long, and is bad for two reasons: constant riding, and particularly jumping, in a small paddock will quickly cut it up and reduce the available feed; and, a pony's paddock should be a place where he can rest and relax, not his principal workplace. So do find out whether your child will be able to ride at Pony Club, apart from rallies, or where other children in the district ride their ponies.

HOW YOU CAN HELP YOUR CHILD

IN THE EARLY STAGES:

Find The Right Pony To Start On

This is a tremendous undertaking. It is no exaggeration to say that there may be times when you will be trusting your child's life, to say nothing of his or her future enjoyment of riding, to this creature. A good first pony is one of the best teachers, and can give a child confidence and an abiding love of horses. Falls are not inevitable — with the right pony and some help in the early stages, they should be rare.

If you have never bought a pony before, do get advice — there are many pitfalls. Avoid in particular the pretty show pony, likely to be much too lively for a beginner; and, young ponies of two, three or four years old. They may be cheap, but they have simply not had time to acquire the necessary experience and reliability (see page 119). The idea of child and pony growing up together, attractive as it may seem, rarely works out in practice.

Pony Club will be only too happy to show you the ropes and to offer advice about suitable ponies and equipment. No instructor wants to have to cope with a keen child on a pony that may be not only unsuitable, but positively dangerous — to its rider and to other children in the class. (The news that you have spent your money unwisely is just as hard for the instructor to hand out as it is for you to accept!)

It is quite likely that somebody at Pony Club will know of a suitable, outgrown pony. If nothing is available locally, enquiries can be made at other clubs, or you can follow up on ponies advertised in newspapers or magazines. However good the pony's 'references', always try to let an experienced person see your child riding it, to make sure that child and pony are physically and temperamentally suited to one another, before you clinch the deal.

12

Buying The Right Equipment

You can often buy the pony's own equipment with it, and this is a good idea, provided it fits well and is in good condition. Failing this, the illustrations and their captions on pages 175 to 186 should help you to make a good choice. Again, if in doubt, do not hesitate to ask advice.

Catching, Grooming And Saddling

Most children like to do things for themselves, and this should be encouraged; but they will need help with picking out the feet, putting on the bridle and tightening the girth.

Check Stirrup Leathers

See that they are level and of the correct length; and help the child to check position and hold the reins correctly.

Lead The Pony

Lead until the child acquires sufficient control to start, stop and guide it, and thereafter be available to help. An older person must always be in the offing when inexperienced children are riding.

Check the Pony's Health and Well-being Daily

Look over the paddock, including water supply; ensure that hay or other feed is available when required, and that the pony's feet are attended to regularly.

Insist On Safety Factors and Consideration For The Pony

Ensure that these are observed from the start. Wearing a hard hat with strap or hat-harness **should be a matter of course** when riding. Footwear too is important around ponies, whether one is mounted or unmounted — bare toes and ponies' feet don't mix well!

Check Saddlery

This must be safe and properly fitted and cared for. It will be inspected at every Pony Club rally; if the instructor suggests some improvement, please do something about it, especially if safety is involved. (Incidentally, messages such as, 'Miss So-and-so says I must have a new saddle' are unlikely, and should be investigated further. It is far more probable that a little extra stuffing or stitching are all that is needed.)

Read This Book Thoroughly

Do this, and you will understand what your child is being taught, and why. If anything is not clear, discuss it with your child's instructor.

As the child becomes more capable and independent, it must obey two safety rules that must never be relaxed:

1. ALWAYS let somebody know where you are going and how long you expect to be away, when you go out for a ride.

2. NEVER practise jumping when you are by yourself, either in the home paddock or anywhere else.

At this stage, when the child is really beginning to enjoy riding, the parent's role can become more difficult. Some parents, often those who always wanted to ride but for one reason or another were prevented from doing so, get carried away and begin to push. They want smarter ponies, a higher class at Pony Club, showing, jumping everything, and all at once. This ultra-competitive attitude spoils the club spirit and turns many promising members into 'pot-hunters'. Do remember it is a sport: at C level at least, let your child ride for the fun of it, and encourage him to measure his achievements on his own personal scale, rather than against others. Later on, if his ability and enthusiasm continue to increase, a different type of pony *will* be needed — plus considerable hard work and application if the child aspires to the higher certificates or to championship standard.

Some parents having bought the pony and equipment, take little or no further interest in their child's riding. But while children are small, someone has to help, or accidents are inevitable.

When they are older, children will, if determined, make out financially one way or another. Many do, by dint of paper-rounds, baby-sitting, lawn-mowing or other means. Pony-keeping is expensive, and children should certainly be encouraged to help out financially if they can. But where so much pleasure is at stake, what a pity if it can't be shared! It is sad if there is no parent there to witness those early triumphs, even if it is only winning a heat of the flag race at a rally.

So do continue to make yourself available to watch and help where you can. If certain things are suggested for practice at Pony Club, encourage this practice. If you consider the pony is being abused in any way, you *must* intervene. Most problems with a good pony come from thoughtlessness or ignorance — try to help to sort things out.

How You Can Help Pony Club

Pony Club, like any other youth movement, needs adults to organise and administer its activities. Many of these adults must have a specialised knowledge of horses and riding, but there are many ways in which the least horsey parent can be of great assistance. Your own professional knowledge — accountancy, carpentry, and so on — may be invaluable, so never be diffident about offering your services, even if you know little about horses.

A word here about Pony Club instructors. They are dedicated people, from all professions and all walks of life, who devote much time and effort to helping children to get the most out of their riding and to take better care of their ponies. The instructors are not only unpaid, but most of them expend time and money attending courses to further their knowledge. Naturally they vary — some are more expert and experienced than others — but there is not one who is not keen to see their pupils improve and enjoy themselves. Instructors really do need parental support and interest in what goes on at Pony Club. Without this support they cannot be expected to continue with what often appears to be a thankless task.

Here are some ways in which all parents can help at rallies:

Be on time. If your child is dependent on you for transport to Pony Club, get him or her there on time. Latecomers are unpopular with instructors as their arrival disrupts a carefully-planned lesson that has already begun.

Be tactful. Take an interest, but *never* interrupt a lesson in progress by talking to the instructor or to your child, or by making audible comments on the sidelines. No system is perfect — if you are really unhappy about what is being done, have a word with the chief instructor or whoever is in charge of the rally, and with your child's instructor after the lesson.

Be helpful. Assist with the games section of a rally. All that is needed here is a person who can keep order and see fair play — especially to the ponies!

Be strong. Dads can help tremendously by forming a roster to set up jumping gear under the instructors' direction, before the rally begins, and by acting as stewards — picking up rails and altering fences — during lessons. Many Pony Club instructors are women, and most jumping-gear is too heavy for them to handle, although they often have to do it. This is not an instructor's job, whether male or female. If fences are to be altered as they should, according to the varying abilities of riders and ponies, help is essential.

Be kitchenhands. Mums can boil the billy, mix the soft drinks and help with the dishes and —

Be carriers. Set up dressage arena and gymkhana equipment, and give a hand with the lighter jumping gear and —

Be stall-minders. Help to run the exchange stall — a great asset to any club in view of the cost of new tack and the fact that children's riding clothes are usually outgrown long before they are outworn.

Before, during and after competition days there are many jobs to be done, including:

Painting and mending jumps and other equipment.

Building showjumping and/or cross-country courses.

Flagging and numbering jumping courses.

Setting up rings, bending-poles, dressage arenas or whatever is needed.

Setting up and running the refreshment stall.

Acting as a steward, timekeeper or writer.

These jobs are easily explained, and it is satisfying to be part of the action.

And, of course, there is always the clearing-up and putting-away afterwards.

In clubs that have their own properties there is always endless work building and maintaining facilities, organising grazing and feeding-out where necessary — all jobs that have to be done by amateur helpers in their spare time.

This list must look somewhat daunting, but it is only intended to suggest ways to help. Don't think you will be involved in all these activities the moment you appear at Pony Club. It is more likely that overworked instructors and officials will hardly have time to greet you. So, do make yourself known, say how much time you have available if you would like to help, and get involved. All this work is helping to increase your own child's knowledge and enjoyment of riding. And you will gain by participating.

As time goes on, do:

Attend meetings. Attend any parents' evenings or activities the club arranges for you: it is frustrating to organise these things and have nobody turn up. Attend the club's annual general meeting.

Read newsletters. Read the club newsletter (perhaps even help to write it?).

You may wish to:

Accept responsibility. Join the club yourself, and accept office on the committee. Attend the annual Pony Club Conference, possibly represent your club as a delegate. Become a perpetual member.

Help instruct. Become an instructor. Courses are available from pre-D level onwards, and the knowledge you gain will be invaluable in helping your own child, even if you never reach the stage of taking rides at Pony Club.

PART I

D CERTIFICATE

TEST SHEET — D CERTIFICATE

Recommended age for D Certificate: 8 or 9 years.

OBJECTIVE

To gain confidence in riding and handling a pony.
To be keen to improve and learn.

RIDING

Mount and dismount (using a mounting block if necessary).
Know the correct position in the saddle.
Show how to hold the reins.
Ride without a leading rein at walk and trot.
Be able to rise to the trot.
Know simple aids for changes of pace and for turning.
Show some physical exercises at halt or walk and know the reasons for doing them.

ROAD SENSE

Know the 'do's and don'ts' for riding on the road.

CARE OF THE PONY

Approach and handle a pony correctly.
Catch pony and put on halter.
Turn pony out into paddock.
Give pony a titbit.
Tie pony up correctly.
Lead pony in hand at walk.
Brush pony over.
Wash the bit (bridle), after riding.
Name simple points of the pony (underlined in chart on page 34).
Name parts of saddle and bridle (underlined in pictures on page 181).

READ

New Zealand Pony Club Manual No 1:
'Riding, D Certificate' (pages 20-34)
'Care of the Pony, D Certificate' (pages 35-39)
'Points of the Horse' (page 34)
'Parts of the Saddle and Bridle' (pages 181 and 176)

2
RIDING: D CERTIFICATE

YOUR FIRST RIDES will be exciting happenings, but try to remember that it is important to start as you mean to go on. Pony Club methods are good ones — even simple things like mounting and dismounting have a right way and a wrong way. The sooner you begin to form the right habits, the easier it will be.

Here is the routine you should always follow for mounting and dismounting from the left side:

Mounting

1. Check that the girths are tight enough — you should just be able to get two fingers under them.
2. Pull both stirrup-irons down, the right one first. Check the approximate length of the stirrups. If you put your clenched fist on the safety-bar of the saddle and stretch the leather along your arm, the base of the stirrup iron should reach your armpit. Make sure both stirrups are the same length. Put the reins over the pony's head.
3. Stand facing the pony's tail, close to his left shoulder. Take up your reins (and whip, if you have one) in the left hand. Have enough contact on the reins to prevent the pony moving off, the right rein slightly shorter. Throw the spare end of the reins over to the far side.
4. Take the back of the stirrup-iron with your right hand, turn it outwards, and put your left foot right 'home' in the iron, with your toe down. That way, you won't poke the pony in the belly with your toe.
5. Put your right hand on the pommel, or on the waist of the saddle on the far side (never on the cantle, as this pulls the saddle over), turn your body to face in towards the pony, and spring up from your right foot, to 'stand' for a moment with both legs together.
6. Swing your right leg over, well clear of the pony's rump, and let yourself down *gently* into the saddle.
7. Put your right foot in the stirrup and take up your reins in both hands. Never allow the pony to move off until you are quite ready.

If your pony is rather tall and you can't reach the stirrup, either use a solid box, step or haybale as a mounting block, or put the pony on the side of a hill so that you are slightly above him, or let the stirrup down.

Dismounting

1. Put the reins (and whip) in the left hand, the end of the reins on the right side of the pony's neck. Take both feet out of the stirrups, put the right hand on the pommel or the pony's shoulder.

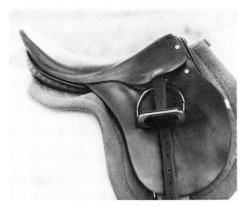

Stirrup correctly run up.

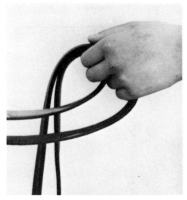

A good way to hold the reins for mounting.

A well-trained pony and a tub to stand on make mounting easier.

A good position. Check with all the points
mentioned on page 23.

2. Lean forward, swing the right leg over well clear of the rump, and
vault off, to land facing forward beside the pony's shoulder.
3. Take the reins over his head and run the stirrups up. If you are not
going to remount at once, slacken the girths a couple of holes.

For mounting and dismounting from the right side, reverse these
instructions.

Never dismount by swinging your leg forward over the pony's
neck. You have to let go of the reins to do this, and if the pony moves
off, you may land on the back of your head.

THE RIDER'S POSITION

The way the rider sits makes all the difference to his riding. It takes
time to achieve a good seat, and much practice.

You should try to sit well down in the centre of the saddle, not on the back of it. Sit straight and tall, and make sure the stirrup leathers are even, and the right length. Your Pony Club instructor will check them for you when you go to a rally, so be sure to notice the number of the hole they should be in.

To check stirrups: get someone to check (by looking from behind) that you are sitting straight, not over to one side, and in the lowest part of the saddle. Take both feet out of the stirrup-irons, stretch your legs well down, and the base of the iron should come just below your ankle-bone. (It is impossible to check this for yourself, because if you look down to see, it makes you lean over to that side.)

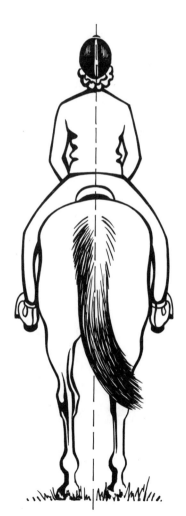

Seen from behind, the rider should be straight and level.

The base of the stirrup-iron should come just below your ankle bone.

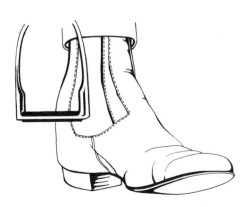

23

Legs

Your thigh and knee should always be against the saddle, but not gripping it tightly, which soon makes you stiff and tired. The inside of your calf should be lightly touching the pony's side, just behind the girth — not gripping. Try to keep your heels down, which may not be easy at first. Keep the stirrup under the ball of your foot (the widest part) and your toe pointing forward. The toe should be directly under the knee.

Hands and Arms

Elbows bent and fairly close to your sides, wrists slightly rounded with knuckles to the front — aim at a straight line from your bent elbow to the pony's mouth.

Holding the Reins

Your little finger may be either inside or outside the rein — if your hands are small, you will probably find it best to have it inside at first. The rein comes up through your hand and out over the top of your first finger, with your thumb flat along the rein. This stops it slipping through your hand. Your fingers should be closed, but not tightly clenched. Never hold the reins in the tips of your fingers, or have them 'upside down', coming into your hand over the top of your first finger. For shortening reins, see page 33, for holding reins in one hand, page 47.

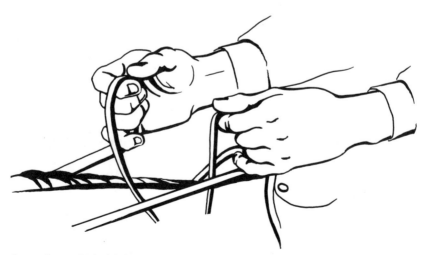

A good way to hold the reins, especially if your hands are small. Little finger inside the rein.

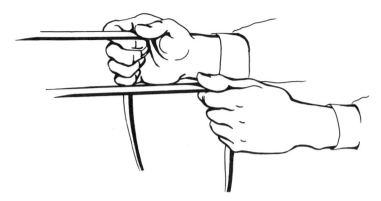

The wrong way — coming into your hand over the top of your first finger.

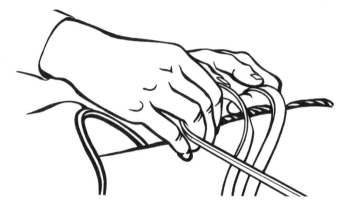

Picking up the reins. Correct — the rein was taken from above and the spare end lies between the rein and the pony's neck. Another good way to hold the reins — little finger outside.

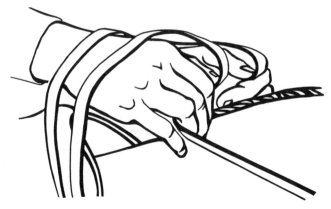

The wrong way. Taking the rein from underneath has caused the spare end to lie over the rider's hand.

STARTING, STOPPING AND GUIDING

The next aim is to get the feel of the pony walking, and to learn to start, stop and guide him. To begin with, it would be best to have someone leading the pony until you get your balance and learn the 'aids', or signals, that tell him what you want him to do.

These aids are given, at this stage, mainly with your legs, hands and voice. Leg aids are given with the inside of your calf, below the knee.

Aids to Walk On

Shorten the reins until you can feel the pony's mouth — make sure the reins are both the same length. Keeping your heels down, close your legs against the pony's sides to make him listen, then give a 'tap, tap', really two sharp nudges, with your legs to tell him to walk on. Let him do this by allowing your hands to follow forward a little.

Position

While he is walking, try to sit still without being stiff, and to let your hands follow the movement of his head and neck, so that he can walk easily. Use your legs if he feels like slowing up. Remember to keep your head up and look where you are going.

Aids to Halt

Be sure to get these aids the right way round. Shoulders back a little, sit tall. Close your legs, then stop following with your hands and squeeze with your fingers, just as you would to get the water out of your face-flannel, several times and just as hard as you need to make it work. Ease your hands as soon as he stops.

Aids to Guide or Turn

To turn to the right: look where you want to go, take your right hand out away from the pony's neck, without pulling back, — (see sketch). This asks him to turn his head and shows him where to go, so your left hand must go forward enough to let him go there. Use both legs to keep him going and, as you improve, try to slide your outside leg — the left one — back about ten centimetres along his side. This helps to control his hindquarters.

Reverse these aids, of course, to turn left. It is always best to walk straight ahead to start with, rather than to turn from a standstill.

Practise starts and stops and turning both ways until you are sure of the aids. As your pony responds, try it on your own in a small, quiet paddock or enclosure. Have someone there to help if necessary. Always try to give your aids smoothly and clearly, without any jerks or snatches, and remember to praise your pony with a 'Good boy', or a pat on the neck when he does what you want.

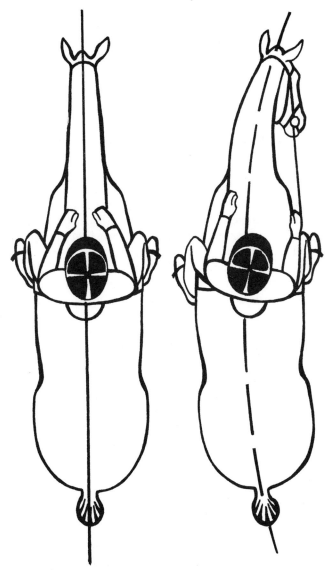

Left: Riding straight ahead. Hands and legs level.

Right: Turning to the right. Right hand opens out, away from the pony's neck, without pulling back. Left hand follows forward. Left leg slides back a little as you use both legs.

TROTTING

Do have someone leading the pony at first. It is less energetic for them if they are mounted on a quiet horse or pony.

Aids To Trot

Exactly the same as for walking. Shorten the reins a little, close your legs and then 'tap, tap', but this time hold the saddle or neck strap with both hands. See that the reins are not *too* short, or the pony won't trot. You may find trotting rather bumpy until you get used to it, so be sure to hold on until you get your balance.

Position

Keep your shoulders back just a little. Keep your knees bent; they are very important shock-absorbers, like car springs. Heels down and head up.

Trot very slowly for just a few metres to start with, and hold the saddle or strap so that your hands don't bounce up and hurt the pony's mouth, or cause you to lose your balance. Have lots of short trots until you find it easy to sit still, and can find enough breath to talk to the person who is leading your pony.

Then try putting the reins in one hand (it helps to tie a knot in them) and holding the saddle with the other hand. You must keep the hand holding the reins down and still. When you can do this, let go of the saddle and take the reins in both hands, but if you lose your balance pop a finger on the saddle quickly or you will jerk the pony's mouth — and he won't like that!

All this time — probably about a week, if you have been riding every day — you have been sitting to the trot. If you have practised properly you should already have quite a good position and be well balanced. If you are riding on a sheepskin without stirrups, you should be quite comfortable and can continue this way for a while yet, but if you have stirrups, now is the time to learn to rise to the trot.

Rising Trot

If the person who has been leading you is mounted, they can show you what rising trot looks like. There are two beats to each stride at the trot, so you rise, slightly forward over your hands, up-down, in time with the one-two beat. Don't push yourself up from the stirrups, but try to let yourself go in rhythm with the pony. Try it standing still to get the timing, which is fairly quick on a small pony. If your sitting trot is steady, you should have little trouble with rising trot. Hold the neckstrap at first if necessary. But *do* practise sitting trot until it is easy and comfortable — it is a mistake to start rising too soon.

Don't try to rise until you can sit to the trot comfortably, like this.

Aids To Walk From The Trot

If you were rising, sit down; head up, shoulders back, close your legs, then squeeze with your fingers, just as you did to halt from the walk. When the pony walks, let your hands follow the movement of his head and neck again, and be ready to use your legs to keep him going.

EXERCISES

Exercises are fun; they also help to improve your balance, make you supple and teach you to control your hands and legs. With someone holding your pony, try these:

Body Bending, Forward

Lean forward and wrap your arms round the pony's neck. Try to keep your feet still — don't let them go back as you lean forward.

Toe-touching

Left hand to left toe, left hand to right toe, both hands, one to each toe, then both hands to one toe — practise it all ways. Remember to keep your feet still!

Airplane Exercise

Both arms out to the side at shoulder height; twist your body to the left and look back along your left arm, over the pony's tail, then do the same to the right. Keep arms level all the time, and legs steady.

Do all these first with stirrups, then with the stirrups crossed in front of the saddle, on the pony's shoulders.

Leg-swinging

Swing your legs, one forward and the other back, from below the knee — let your toes hang down, so that the leg will be loose and relaxed. Good for a rest, and for stiff knees.

Ankle-turning

Turn both feet up, in, down, out several times. Quite hard work, but very good for suppling your ankles, and so making it easier to keep your heels down.

Try both these last two while keeping your hands in riding position, as if you were holding the reins. See how still you can keep your hands. Do these last two with stirrups crossed.

Now an exercise for the daredevils — **Round The World.** Swing your right leg over the pony's neck, sit sideways; then left leg over his rump, facing the tail, right leg over again, then left leg over his neck and you're 'round the world'. Do it both ways — fun to see how quick you can be. When you can do it easily 'with hands', try it with your arms folded. Have someone hold your pony at first.

As you improve, try some of these exercises (but not 'Round The World' yet!) at the walk.

GOING TO PONY CLUB

By this time you should be feeling quite confident at the walk and trot; able to start and stop easily and to turn your pony in any direction. You will now be ready to go to Pony Club and join a 'ride' there, where you will do all these things with others; this is much more fun. Listen to your instructor and make your pony listen to you — he may be excited, too. Remember, ponies sometimes kick, so be sure to keep yours away from other ponies' heels. You are sure to

Exercises are fun! 'Round the world' together.

have games at Pony Club, and, if you have practised everything you have been taught, you should both enjoy them enormously.

CANTER

As your balance and control improve, you will be ready to canter. How you start depends on your pony; if he is lazy, start by cantering towards the gate of the paddock; if he is a little keen, then go away from the gate. Start on the flat, or slightly uphill, if possible, on a straight line, and always in a paddock. A mounted person alongside helps a lot.

Aids To Canter

Sit to the trot, hold the saddle with one hand, give just the same leg aids as you do to trot — close the legs, and 'tap, tap', fairly sharply if the pony is inclined to be lazy. If he just trots faster, bring him back to a steady pace before trying again.

Position

The canter will feel like a rather lively rocking-horse at first, but *you* don't have to rock, as you did on the wooden one! Sit as still as you can, and don't forget to breathe. Just canter a few paces, then back to trot and walk. Do hold the saddle, or your hands may come up and make you lose your balance. Cantering is fun, but too much can cause upsets and is hard work for your pony. Don't be in a hurry — short spells, and always on grass, never on the road or the roadside, or on any hard surface.

Hold the saddle or neckstrap for your first canters, or your hands may come up and make you lose your balance.

RIDING ON THE ROAD: DO'S AND DON'TS
Do's

1. As always, WEAR YOUR HARD HAT, and have a bridle on your pony.
2. Keep to the left at all times, unless there is a really wide grass verge on the right.
3. Ride at a walk or a *steady* trot.
4. If several of you are riding together, keep together (but not abreast), and *all on the same side.*
5. When crossing, halt, look both ways, cross smartly at right angles when all is clear. If there are several of you, all turn and cross together.
6. Say 'Thank you', if motorists slow up for you. Consider other people on the road.
7. Get back to the paddock before dusk.

Dont's

1. **Don't go** out without your parent's knowledge and permission, and until you are fully in control of your pony.

2. **Don't ride** on footpaths or mown grass verges, except in emergency.

3. **Don't ride** more than two abreast. Single file is safer if the road is narrow or the traffic is heavy.

4. **Don't canter** on the road — even when you *can* canter! It is dangerous, and very bad for your pony's legs.

5. **Don't take** chances on bridges or narrow cuttings. On a busy road you should not attempt to negotiate them without an experienced escort.

By this time your riding should be good enough for you to sit your D Certificate. In fact, you don't have to canter for D, but it is just as well to have done a little at this stage.

But don't forget there is another side to owning ponies — the care of your pony. Ponies have to be looked after every day — they are not like bicycles that you can put away in a shed until you want them again. The Test Sheet on page 19 shows you the very simple requirements for D Certificate. You must really be able to *do* the things like tying up and brushing your pony over, not just know about them. There will be many things you will need help with, but take a pride in doing as much as you possibly can do yourself for your pony.

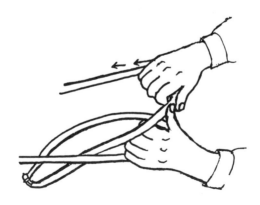

To shorten the right rein, take hold of the right rein between your left thumb and first finger, then slide your right hand down to the required length. Reverse the process when you shorten the left rein.

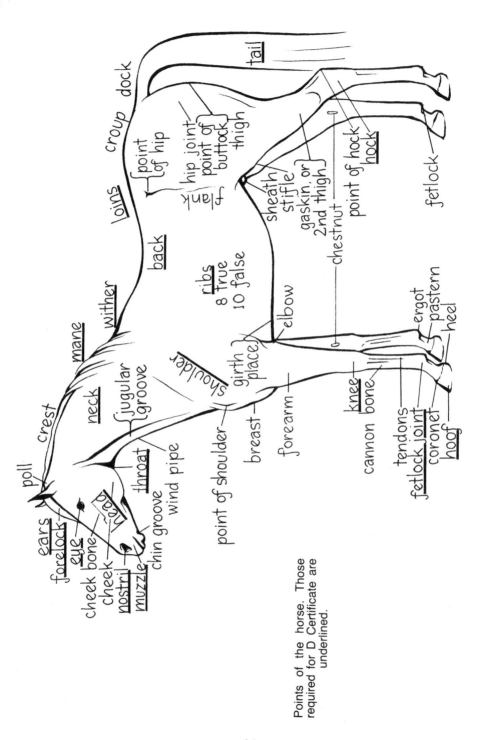

Points of the horse. Those required for D Certificate are underlined.

34

3
CARE OF THE PONY: D CERTIFICATE

CATCHING

IT IS BEST to catch your pony every day, even if you are not going to ride him. You should check him to see that all is well. The fact that you don't always expect him to work after you have caught him will make it easier to catch him another time.

When you go to catch him, have the halter over your shoulder, with rope attached. Take a piece of bread or other titbit with you. Go to within calling distance and see if he will come to you. If you show him the bread, he will probably come quite happily. Give him part of the titbit, keeping your hand quite flat, so that he does not nip your thumb. Then slide the rope over his neck, put on the halter and give him the remainder of the titbit.

A titbit keeps the pony occupied while you slip the rope over his neck.

With a shy pony it is best for someone he knows to go out quietly and alone to catch him. With every pony it is important not to run at him, or shout, or wave the halter about. If your pony is grazing with several others, you may have to catch him without the titbit. Give it to him after you have left the paddock; then there is no risk of the others trying to bully your pony.

TURNING OUT

Once inside the paddock, shut the gate and lead the pony about five metres away. Then turn him towards the gate, slip the halter off and let him move quietly away. Chasing him off will make him much harder to catch next time.

If your pony has to have his halter left on to assist in catching, be sure that it fits properly (see illustration on page 39) and that someone sees him every day in case it has slipped over one ear or is rubbing him.

It is not a good idea to catch or turn your pony out using a bridle. It can easily get damaged, and when taking it off, it can catch on his teeth if he pulls away. This would make him hard to bridle.

TYING-UP

Careless tying-up causes many accidents to ponies and people. Always tie to something firm, such as a solid post or rail. Never tie to anything movable, like a jump stand, or to a wire in the fence. It is best to tie to a small loop of twine or string attached to the solid post or rail; this is especially important if the pony is inclined to pull back, or you are on somebody else's property so that nothing will get broken. Use a quick-release knot, as shown. Don't have the rope too long, or he may put his foot over it and hurt himself. He should just be able to get his nose to the ground. For the knot see opposite page.

Never tie your pony up by the bridle. The probable effects of that would be a broken bridle and a pony with a very sore mouth.

APPROACHING AND HANDLING

Ponies are rather nervous animals, so always speak as you approach them. Approach from the side, towards the shoulder, never from behind. When you handle a pony, be quite firm and sure. Do not suddenly grab a leg or make a stab with your brush or your hand at any part of him. One of his defences is to kick, and he may do this before he realises that it was you and not an enemy, or a fly who has just prodded a ticklish spot!

36

Depending on your size, you may need some help with brushing your pony. For a small person, a small brush with a strap across the back is much easier to handle than a dandy brush. If the bristles of the brush are fairly soft, it may also be used on the mane and tail. A dandy brush is usually too hard to use on mane and tail. In addition, you will need a plastic or rubber curry comb and a hoof pick (see page 146).

Start brushing behind the ear on the left side. Hold the brush in your left hand while you brush the neck, shoulder, chest and foreleg. Halfway along the pony's body, change hands and do the rest of his body and hindquarters.

Use the brush briskly, with a to-and-fro action, if necessary, to loosen dried mud or sweat. Brush across, not against, the lie of the hair, but always finish with the lie of the hair. Reverse this when you do the right side. Get used to handling the brush in either hand from the start. Undo the noseband of the halter and brush the pony's face carefully. Finish by brushing his mane and tail.

Never use the curry comb on face, mane or tail. Use it to help

A quick-release knot.

Thorough brushing around the girth area is essential. The pony is well tied up, with the correct length of rope. Note the loop of binder twine and quick-release knot. The halter is a little low.

37

remove dried mud, or when the winter coat starts to come out in the spring. If the mud is wet, it is best to let it dry before trying to brush it; a rub over with a handful of hay or straw can help to dry him more quickly.

The pony's feet must be picked out, but get help with these for a start. It is very important to see that the feet are picked out before you ride, and brush away all mud, at least from where the saddle, girth and bridle go. Otherwise your pony will be very uncomfortable, and could go lame or get a sore back or a girth gall.

After your ride, be sure to brush out these same places before turning the pony out. Better still, brush him over completely. A rub with a towel will help to dry any damp spots. Always wear solid footwear around ponies. Never sit, kneel or crawl underneath a pony — bend or squat down when you brush his legs.

LEADING IN HAND

Halter or bridle. Ponies are usually led from the left side, but you should practise it from both sides. Leading from the left side, hold the rope or reins in your right hand, with the knuckles on top, about 30cm from the halter or bit, the other end in your left hand, together with your whip, if you are carrying one. Face forward, stay level with the pony's shoulder, and as you walk off say 'Walk on', smartly. Do not turn round to face the pony or try to drag him along. To turn him, push him away from you so that you stay on the outside. Never pull him round you — he could easily tread on your toes! Notice in the picture how the rope is held; it is dangerous to wrap or loop it round your hand.

POINTS OF THE HORSE

Ponies do have shoulders and knees, but not, for instance, ankles; these are called fetlock joints. The chart on page 34 shows all the points of the horse. The ones you need to know for D Certificate are underlined.

Parts of the saddle and bridle are shown on pages 181 and 176.

There is a lot to learn about looking after ponies. They cannot tell us when they are tired, sore or hungry; we have to learn to recognise the signs. If you are in doubt about anything, for example, a scratch or a cough, however small it may seem, always ask for help.

Good handling of rope, and pony leading well. Note correctly-fitting halter and thick lead-rope.

Bottom left: This way of holding the rope is also acceptable.

PART II

C CERTIFICATE

TEST SHEET: C CERTIFICATE

Recommended age for C Certificate: 11 or 12 years.

OBJECTIVE

To attain a firm seat, independent of the reins, on the flat and over small fences.

To know, and be able to apply, correct aids for simple movements.

To be in control of the pony at all times.

To understand the Road Code, and to show common sense and courtesy when out and about with a pony.

To have a knowledge of the daily care and working of the pony.

RIDING

Turnout of pony and rider.

Mount and dismount from either side.

Know the reasons for maintaining the correct position in the saddle.

Show a reasonably steady and correct position at walk, trot (rising and sitting) and canter. Ride without stirrups at walk and trot, holding saddle if necessary.

Be able to rise to the trot on either diagonal, as required.

Hold reins correctly in one or both hands.

Handle a whip correctly, and know how and when to use it.

Alter stirrups when mounted.

Adjust girths when mounted.

Understand the meaning of the word 'aids'.

Know the aids for, and be able to carry out the following movements:
    (a) Simple transitions.
    (b) Turns and circles.
    (c) Canter on a named leg on a circle.

Walk and trot on a long rein.

Ride up and down hill.

Show how to open and shut a gate, mounted or unmounted at candidate's choice.

Have control of the pony in the school and in the open.

Have some knowledge of the pony's paces and the way he should go.

Ride over poles on the ground or cavalletti at walk and trot.

Show a steady position and contact over small fences.

Jump a short course of varied fences.

Jump small fences on slopes, and small ditches.

(Maximum height for C Certificate fences, 65cm.)

Know the rules and correct signals when riding on the road.

Know how to behave when riding on private property, in public places, and at Pony Club.

KNOWLEDGE OF PONY CLUB

Know the names of the District Commissioner and Branch head instructor.

Know the name and location of one other branch of Pony Club.

CARE OF THE PONY

Paddocking

Requirements of a pony at grass.

What to look for when choosing a paddock.

Elementary care of pony paddocks.

Care of pony with the change of seasons.

Feeding

Elementary watering, feeding and exercise.

Knowledge of feedstuffs *as applied to own pony*.

Handling

Show due regard for safety factors when handling ponies.

Lead pony in hand at walk and trot, turn about.

Know how to take a quiet pony in and out of a float.

Grooming

Know the reasons for grooming.

Show how to use a dandy brush, body brush, curry comb, sponges (for eyes, nose and dock), and hoof pick.

Care of the mane and tail.

Pick up and pick out the feet.

Care of pony before and after riding.

Care of grooming kit.

Shoeing

Recognise a cast, loose, worn or sprung shoe, excessively long foot, risen clench, shoe pressing on seat of corn.

In a newly-shod foot, recognise very high clench, excessive rasping of wall — know what action to take.

Recognise simple types of shoes — e.g. fore, hind, concave, road shoe.

Health

Know the indications of good and bad health in the pony.

Recognise when a pony is lame.

Treatment of minor wounds and injuries.

Some knowledge of possible causes of poor condition — worms, bots, malnutrition, teeth needing attention.

Know the obvious symptoms of: colic, laminitis, grass staggers, coughs, colds, lice, ticks (where prevalent) and ringworm, and know what immediate action to take.

Medicine chest (up to present requirements).

Know when to seek adult advice.

SADDLERY AND EQUIPMENT

Be able to saddle and bridle.

Correct fitting of *own pony's* saddle and bridle. Also curb chain and martingale, if used.

Know the name and action of *own pony's* bit.

Put on and take off a cover.

Elementary care and cleaning of saddlery and covers.

GENERAL KNOWLEDGE

Points of the horse, colours and markings.

Description of ponies.

Measurement of ponies.

READ

New Zealand Pony Club Manual, No. 1.
Riding, D Certificate.
Riding C Certificate.
Out And About With Your Pony.
Jumping.
Care of the Pony, D Certificate.
Care of the Pony, C Certificate.
Saddlery and Equipment.

4
RIDING: C CERTIFICATE

WHEN you have gained your D Certificate you will know that you have made a good start on the right lines. Your next objective is to improve your seat. You want it to become firm and steady and independent of the reins — which have nothing to do with keeping you on the pony's back. As your seat improves, you will be able to give clearer aids, or signals, to your pony, and this will make for a better partnership between you.

By now you should be beginning to see the reasons for the things you were told when you started riding. For instance:

SEAT

Sit deep in the lowest part of the saddle. This gets you as close as possible to the pony, and keeps you in balance with him. If you sit on the back of the saddle, it is uncomfortable for the pony, and you will feel as though you are being 'left behind'.

LEGS

Thigh and knee close to the saddle. Ready to grip *only* in emergency — otherwise they must be relaxed and supple.

Inside of the calf touching the pony's side. Ready to apply your leg aids lightly and instantly, as needed. If the leg is away from the pony, it often acts too hard and too late.

Toes as straight as you can. If you turn your toes out it brings your knee away from the saddle, and encourages you to grip with your calf. Toes turned in bring the calf right away from the pony's side, and make you very stiff.

Heels down. You must know by now what happens when your heels come up. Your knees come up, too, and all balance and steadiness are lost. Keeping your heels down makes your calf muscles firm, so that you can give clearer leg aids.

Stirrup under the ball of the foot. Helps to keep your toes up, and gives more spring in the ankle than you have with the foot 'home'.

UPPER PART OF THE BODY

Sit straight, keep your shoulders level, and make sure your leathers are the same length, otherwise your pony will find it harder to go straight or to turn when you want him to. Sit tall, but don't hollow your back — then you will be able to use your back and seat as

45

A: A good position and length of leather. Note the line through the rider's ear, shoulder, hip and heel, and the straight line from elbow to bit.

B: Stirrups too short, pushing the rider's seat on to the back of the saddle. The legs have shot forward, making it impossible to apply the aids correctly.

C: Stirrups too long. The rider is 'on his fork', in a weak and unbalanced position.

aids when the time comes. Looking where you are going means just that — if you are turning towards a jump, for example, then look that way. If you are looking ahead, you will be thinking ahead, and have much more chance of getting where you want to go.

HANDS AND ARMS

All the joints at elbow, wrist and fingers must be relaxed. If you ride with stiff elbows and the back of your hand on top, your hands will be hard and heavy, and you will never be able to give sympathetic aids.

The first thing is to try to get your hands still, with a light, even contact on the pony's mouth. At the walk, his head moves a little and your hands must move with it. His head should be quite steady at trot and canter, and so should your hands.

You should be able to hold the reins correctly by now, but do practise handling them — dropping them on to the buckle, picking them up, lengthening and shortening them, putting both reins into one hand; all done smoothly, without any jerks. Never forget that at the other end of those reins is a steel bit, lying on your pony's lips, tongue, and the bars of his mouth (the stretch of bare gum between his front and back teeth).

Reins in one hand. The right rein crosses over the left, with the forefinger in between.

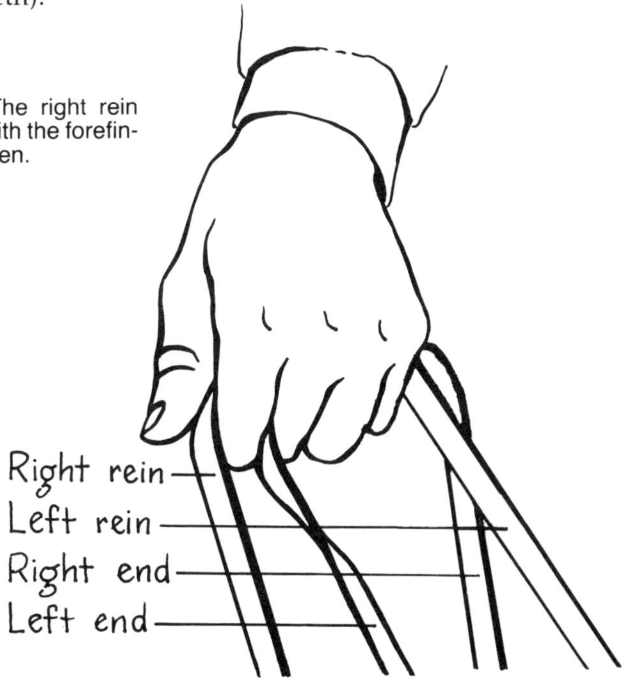

Right rein
Left rein
Right end
Left end

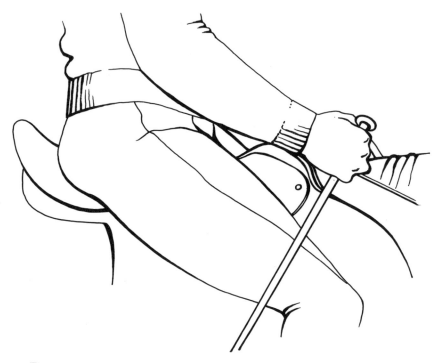

The whip is held close to the knob, and should lie just above your knee.

It is now time to get used to carrying a whip. You should always carry it, for reasons which will be explained later. It should lie in the middle of your thigh, not down the pony's shoulder, or up under your arm or sticking straight out to the side. Properly held, you will find it is a great help in maintaining the correct hand position. It is important to get used to holding and handling your whip equally well with either hand, and changing it from one hand to the other.

If you find it hard to keep your hands still, it is probably because your balance is not quite right. Perhaps you are sitting too upright in rising trot, going up and down rather than forward and down, over your hands. In canter, you may have a stiff back and be rocking your body too much, which makes your hands jerk at every step. Try resting your little fingers on top of the pony's shoulders, even if you have to lean forward slightly to get them there. When they begin to stay there easily you can raise your hands and sit up straighter. Your bent elbow and straight line from elbow to bit is the best guide to the right height of hand for you. Your hands should never be higher than your elbows, and normally they should be about 10-15cm apart. Until you can keep your hands still and independent, you cannot use them effectively.

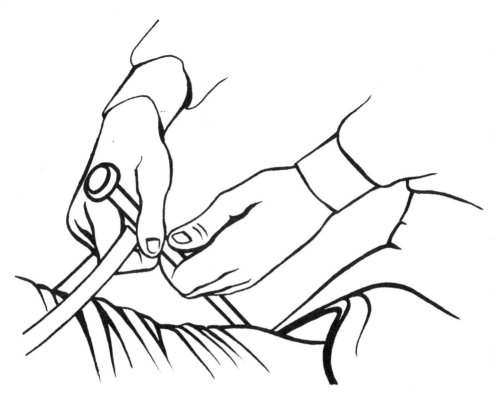

Changing the whip from right to left. Put both reins into the right hand (see page 47) with whip. Then lift right thumb for an instant to release whip, and lift it cleanly over the pony's neck before taking back the left rein.

EXERCISES

Keep on practising the exercises you learned before D Certificate. They are excellent for improving your balance and suppleness and giving you an independent seat, so that you can keep your hands and lower legs still, without any stiffness.

Here are some new ones: Arm circling; hands on hips, body turning keeping the head to the front; heel clicking, 'twisting round'; vaulting on and off. You will learn all these at Pony Club.

Trotting Without Stirrups

To begin with, *always* hold the saddle, and have short, steady trots. Use the inside hand on the pommel to pull your seat forward and down, so that you are really sitting on your seat bones. You should feel that you are *almost* leaning back. Be careful to keep the hand holding the reins down and still. Don't grip, try to stretch down and relax, keeping knees and ankles well bent. When you feel comfortable

Heel clicking. Good for balance and coordination.
Ponies must be held in exercises like this until they are used to them.

It takes practice to develop a really deep seat.

This rider is well on the way, although her knee is a little stiff.

and well balanced, try holding with just one finger; if you can still keep steady, let go and let your arm hang down to your side. You may find at first that your shoulders come forward and your seat slips back; or your hands may come up, which will make you bump about — most uncomfortable for you and the pony. If anything goes wrong, just hold the saddle again until you regain your balance.

It takes time, patience and persistence to acquire the knack of doing a good sitting trot. As you progress with your riding, you will realise more and more how important it is. Don't try to do exercises at the trot just yet.

Trotting With Stirrups

Practise sitting trot with stirrups, too — holding the saddle to begin with. If you keep losing your stirrups, this shows that you are gripping upwards. Try to stretch down, so that the weight goes down through your bent knee into your heel, behind the stirrup iron.

Pony and rider going well. Note rider's head up, body slightly forward in rising trot, straight line from elbow to bit.

51

Standing Trot

This is a useful exercise; it helps to get the position of your lower leg right. The idea is to maintain the position as for the 'up beat' of rising trot. Rest your hand on the pony's mane, not the saddle, at first; keep your knees bent. When you get your balance, try it with your hand on your hip. If your feet are stuck out in front, you will find you just can't get there; if they are too far back, you will flop forward on the pony's neck. It is almost impossible to do the exercise at all unless you have your heels down.

As you practise these exercises, you should find that your stirrups feel too short. This is good; it shows that your seat is getting deeper. By all means let the stirrups down a hole or two. With feet out of the stirrups and legs stretched down, the base of the stirrup iron should now be approximately halfway between your ankle bone and the instep of the boot.

The base of the stirrup-iron should now be about halfway between the ankle bone and the instep of the boot.

Diagonals. This rider is using the left diagonal. She is sitting as the left foreleg and the right hind leg are on the ground. She will rise as they go forward.

DIAGONALS

You should now start to learn about diagonals, so that you get into the habit of using them correctly. At the trot, the pony springs from one diagonal pair of legs to the other. The left fore and right hind are called the 'left diagonal', the right fore and left hind, the 'right diagonal'.

When you are rising to the trot you will be using one diagonal or the other. If you rise as the pony's left shoulder goes forward and sit as it comes back, you will be on the left diagonal — a quick glance down should show you which shoulder you are following, until you get the knack of feeling this without needing to look.

When riding out, it makes it less tiring for the pony if you change the diagonal at regular intervals. You do this by sitting for two beats together — up, down, down, up. Use the outside diagonal on circles or when working in a school — this helps to keep your pony better balanced and he will bend more easily. Try to remember to change the diagonal whenever you change direction.

POSITION AT CANTER

All your work at the sitting trot will help tremendously with the canter. Try to relax your back and let your body go with the movement of the pony, without any exaggerated rocking to and fro.

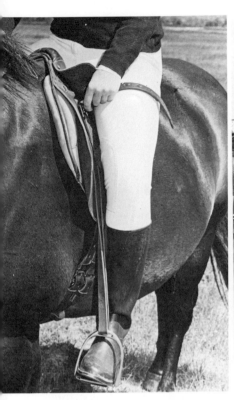 

Left: Altering stirrups. Put the whip and reins in the opposite hand. Undo the buckle with your thumb and first finger, keeping it close to the safety bar. *Never* take your foot out of the stirrup — maintaining some tension on the leather makes it easier to guide the tongue of the buckle into the required hole.

Right: Tightening the girth. Keep your foot in the stirrup, the leg in front of the saddle flap. The right hand holds the flap up, the left hand adjusts the buckle.

ALTERING STIRRUPS AND GIRTHS WHEN MOUNTED

It is most important to get into the habit of making these alterations correctly, without taking your foot out of the stirrup, in either case.

To Sum Up: You should have a good idea by now of what you are trying to do, and why. You should be able to keep a good position for most of the time, though you may still lose it in moments of stress. You will find that the better your position is, the better you can communicate with your pony and the more you can expect to get out of your riding, so it's well worth working at it! Five or ten minutes practice every time you ride can make an amazing difference.

THE AIDS

You already know one meaning of the word aids — signals to tell your pony what you want him to do. It also means the things you use to give those signals. There are two kinds of aids, natural and artificial.

Natural aids are your back, seat, legs, hands, and voice.

Artificial aids are whips, spurs, and various articles of saddlery, such as martingales and dropped nosebands.

Natural Aids

Back and seat. At first, just try to sit tall and keep your shoulders back before you apply leg or hand aids for a transition (a change of pace) or for a change of direction. Always sit down for the first few strides when you start trotting. When you go from trot to walk or to canter, sit down, because you can't possibly use your seat when you are rising to the trot, and you can't use your legs so efficiently either. Gradually, as your seat gets deeper and steadier, you will begin to feel the swing of your pony's back and the movement of his hind legs through your seat bones. This sense of 'feel' is a big step forward in riding. As your position strengthens, you will be able to make use of your back and seat as aids.

Legs create impulsion or energy in the pony, drive him forward when necessary, and control his hindquarters and the bend or straightness of his body.

Hands control the energy created by the seat and legs, by allowing the pony to continue at the same pace or to go into a faster one, or by checking him. They place his head the way he is going and control his forehand.

Voice is mainly used to let your pony know if he is doing the right thing in response to your other aids. It can keep his attention; praise and encourage him; reassure him if he is frightened or doubtful, or reprimand him if he is wrong through wilfulness. People are often very selfconscious about talking to their ponies, and this is a pity, because it does so much to foster the partnership between rider and pony. That partnership is what riding is all about.

Artificial aids

Whip. As soon as you can manage your reins reasonably well, you should always carry a whip, so that you will have something to back up your leg if your pony doesn't obey it promptly.

Spurs should not be used until you reach a much more advanced stage of riding. Wearing spurs, you must be able to keep your legs steady at all times, so that you won't jab the pony with them by mistake.

A dropped noseband can be useful with some ponies (page 177). Other 'extras' should not be needed, at least for the time being. If in doubt, ask your Pony Club instructor.

AIDS FOR INCREASE AND DECREASE OF PACE

Upward Transitions

Halt to walk. First call the pony to attention; sit tall, look where you want to go, feel his mouth. Close your legs, then a light 'tap, tap' with your legs. As he responds, your hands allow him to go, and follow the movement of his head and neck as he walks on. If you lose contact with his mouth, you cannot control his pace or direction, and he may be unbalanced as he goes forward.

Some ponies may not obey light leg aids. If yours doesn't, *don't* kick, use your whip, otherwise he will quickly become 'leg-proof' and take no notice of your legs at all. The whip should be used on his ribs, as close as possible to your leg, not on his shoulder. To use the whip, you must put your reins in one hand; if you use the whip with your hand on the rein, you will jerk his mouth.

Next time you ask him to walk on, have your whip ready behind your leg, and use it sharply if he disobeys again. Use your voice to tell him to 'Walk on'. Be ready to give with your hand to let him go. Remember to praise him when he gets it right. Try to finish with a nice, free 'walk on' without having to use the whip.

Walk to trot. Shorten your reins, because the pony carries his head higher at the trot. Use the aids as above, remembering to sit down for the first few trot strides.

Trot to canter. Sit to the trot, shoulders back, close, tap, tap with your legs, give enough with your hands to let him canter. 'Cantering on a named leg' is explained and the aids given on page 61.

Downward Transitions

Walk to halt. Sit tall, close your legs with a light even feel to keep the pony's hocks under him and push him up to your hand. Stop following with the hands and use them with that intermittent squeezing action, giving when he gives and closing when he resists, until the pony halts. If he doesn't want to stop, push your heels down harder, keep your shoulders back so that he doesn't pull you up his neck, and close your hands very firmly. On no account give to him until he gives to you, but as soon as he gives the slightest bit, your hand must acknowledge this by relaxing for an instant, then asking again. Never snatch or saw roughly at your pony's mouth. Don't forget the praise when he does halt.

Trot to walk. Sit to the trot, then use legs and hands as above. Push the pony forward actively and let your hands follow as soon as he walks.

Canter to trot. Aids as above. You may find this transition rather bumpy at first, until you get the knack of keeping your heels down,

Downward transitions. A carefully-ridden transition. Notice the rider's back and the soft closing of her legs and fingers. The pony is steady and attentive, and quite well balanced for this stage of training.

How **NOT** to do them. This rider shows us what happens when you don't sit down and close your legs. The pony has lost his balance and is leaning on her hands.

and all your joints relaxed. By all means hold the saddle if you feel unsteady.

At this stage, practise these simple transitions, from one pace to the next. Don't try to skip a pace, by going from walk to canter or from trot to halt, for example.

All hand, no leg! This rider shows other faults. Her hands are stiff and too high, with the knuckles on top. She has used them first instead of last.

AIDS FOR TURNS

At first, you used what is called an 'open rein', taking your inside hand out from the pony's neck, when you were turning. As you get the feel of using your aids, you will find that you can gradually cut down the amount of 'opening'. You will begin to turn more by 'asking' with the inside hand, while 'giving' with the outside hand enough to let the pony turn, but not enough to let him bend his neck too much, or go faster. Your legs will have to be used quite firmly to push him up to this 'asking' inside hand. The outside leg must go back to control his hindquarters and stop him swinging them out as he turns.

CIRCLES

The object of circles is to make your pony supple, so that he can bend his spine equally both ways. This improves his balance, and makes him a better 'ride'.

Aids

Be sure to sit straight — don't lean in — and look where you want to go. Place the pony's head to the inside so that you can just see his eyelashes, using a squeezing action with your fingers and a very slightly open rein; give enough with your outside hand to let him turn his head this much, but no more.

The outside leg slides back about 10cm to control his quarters. This is the supporting leg and, apart from helping lightly to keep him going, acts only if the quarters swing out. It is most important to get into the habit of keeping the outside leg back when you are turning or circling.

The inside leg is the acting leg, used just behind the girth; it not only creates impulsion, but also the bend in his body, and keeps the pony out on the circle. If he is stiff, this leg, possibly backed up by your whip, becomes even more important. Remember to keep your heel down, and use the inside of the calf with a light tapping action, rather than a tight squeeze.

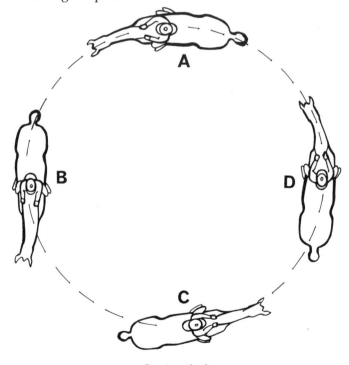

On the circle.
A: A good bend through the whole length of the pony. **B:** The rider is pulling the outside rein to keep the pony out, so he *cannot* bend correctly. **C:** The pony is not bending at all. No aids, he's not being asked to! **D:** Too much neck bend, hindquarters swinging out. No outside leg.

59

The idea is to get the pony to bend evenly from poll to tail, so that his hind feet follow exactly in the tracks of his forefeet. He should be bent like a banana round your inside leg. So your circles must be quite big to start with, certainly not less than 20 metres across, because, of course, the smaller the circle the more he will have to bend his body. Don't keep circling for too long — one or two good ones at a time is plenty.

If the pony 'falls in' (makes the circle too small and does not bend properly) use your whip behind your inside leg. Touch him very gently at first, gradually tapping harder with whip and leg together while restraining him from going faster, until you feel him edge out and bend his back a little more. Immediately praise him with your voice while he is doing what you want; stop using the whip, but keep it close behind your leg, ready if he doesn't continue to obey the leg on its own.

Never try to keep him out by pulling the outside rein or crossing your inside hand over his neck. Make sure that the inside hand doesn't pull back towards your stomach. Both reins must be the same length, don't shorten either of them. The only exception to this is when you are using your whip to reinforce your leg, and have both reins in the outside hand. In this case, the inside rein should be a little shorter.

Teaching the pony to obey the rider's inside leg, so that he keeps out and bends on the circle.

If you use your whip like this, you will find that your pony will soon learn to listen to your leg aids, and will obey them more and more easily. Nearly all ponies are stiffer on one side than the other. You will have to make your aids very clear on your pony's stiff or 'hard' side, but it is always best to start on his 'soft' side, to give him time to warm up and get going.

When you have made some progress at this, and your pony is beginning to bend nicely without your having to use your whip, you will find that he feels smoother and more responsive. It will be much easier to get him to canter on a given leg, which comes next.

AIDS FOR THE CANTER ON A NAMED LEG ON A CIRCLE OR TURN

If you watch a pony cantering, you will see that his legs on one side appear to be going in front of his legs on the other side. The pony in the picture is leading on the left fore — his two left legs are obviously leading the right ones at this moment.

On a turn or circle, a pony should always lead on the inside leg, otherwise he will be unbalanced and could hit himself, stumble or fall. So it is important to learn the aids to tell him which leg you want him to lead on. You may find it better to start to the left, as many ponies lead more easily on the left fore.

Canter. This pony is leading on the left foreleg. The rider's leg position is good, but she is leaning slightly forward, so the pony is a little heavy. Nevertheless, they look a happy pair.

On a fairly large circle, or coming into a corner in the school, check that the pony's head is placed to the inside. Check that your outside leg is back, controlling his quarters. Trot a few strides sitting, keep your shoulders and outside leg back as you give your leg aids in the usual way. Don't lean forward or look down to see if he is on the right leg — this is one of the hardest habits to overcome, and puts the pony right off balance. Much better to get somebody to tell you at first; with practice, you will soon learn to feel which leg is leading.

If the pony goes on the wrong leg, bring him back at once to the trot or walk, saying 'No' as you do so. Check the bend again, check your position, and be sure to use both legs as you ask him to strike off. If he is still wrong, bring him back again, saying 'No', a little more sharply this time; put your whip in the outside hand, and use it to reinforce the outside leg. Make much of the pony as soon as he gets it right, then keep him going for a while, praising him all the time he is doing what you want.

It could happen that your pony goes 'disunited'. This means that he is leading with one foreleg and the opposite hind leg. This is a most uncomfortable, twisting movement, which you will recognise quite easily once you have felt it. If it happens, check him at once; correct in the same way as for leading on the wrong leg.

Sometimes ponies have been allowed to get into the habit of always leading with the same leg. If, in the early stages, you find it very hard to get your pony to lead on one leg or the other, try riding directly away from the gate, then turning rather sharply round a post or other marker, towards his difficult side, at the same time using your whip behind the outside leg as you push him into the canter. Again, keep him going and praise him when he gets it right.

YOUR PONY'S PACES AND THE WAY HE SHOULD GO

If you are to enjoy your riding as you should, you want your pony to go kindly, calmly but freely in all his paces. All the work you have been doing — improving your seat and position, and applying your aids for turns, circles and transitions — will make it easier for him to go well because you will be so much steadier, and your aids will be clearer.

Each of the paces has its own rhythm, like music. The walk is four-time, the trot two-time, and the canter three-time. You have to find the pony's best speed in each of these paces; not so fast that he is scuttling along like an agitated beetle; not so slow that he feels lazy and half-asleep. If he doesn't do so already, you have to teach him to keep that regular beat at all times, not only on the flat, on straight lines, turns and circles and changes of direction, but also up and down hill, and in his jumping.

Now, when you are practising, keep going for a longer period at one pace, and concentrate on this idea of rhythm.

The trot is the simplest pace and the best one to start with. Ride round your paddock, or along a quiet road where there is not much traffic to distract you. At the trot, the strides should be long and springy. *Don't go too fast*, or the strides will be come short and choppy — the pony should feel energetic, but not hurried. If he tries to go faster, say, 'No, steady,' and close your fingers until he comes back to the right speed, then immediately reward him by giving (relaxing fingers). If he slows down, use your legs with a light, tapping action, and, if necessary use your whip also, until he is going forward actively again. It helps to count, 'One, two, one, two' under your breath, or hum a marching tune to help you keep time. If he keeps the rhythm without having to be corrected for about a minute at first, bring him back to the walk and give him a long rein and a pat on the neck. Gradually build up the time you ask him to maintain the rhythm.

Next, work on the walk. The four beats should be clear and distinct, and the pace should be energetic — someone walking alongside should find it quite hard to keep up. When a pony walks well, swinging his back and neck and bringing his hocks well under him, he is using every muscle in his body. It is a wonderful pace for getting him fit, when you begin to think about hunting and competitive riding. The print of his hindfoot should come well past the print of his forefoot on the same side; you can check this by looking at his hoof prints on soft ground, or anyone watching can easily tell you. Many ponies trot too fast and walk too slowly, so don't make that mistake — he must march, not mooch!

When these two paces are improving, try — in the paddock only — letting your reins out until you are out of contact with the pony's mouth. See if you can guide him on large circles and changes of direction without using the reins at all. This will show whether he is really getting the idea of keeping that even pace, and whether he understands when you are using your legs to guide him, not to increase the pace. When you can do it, you will know that you are using your leg aids well, and that the partnership between you is improving.

The walk on a long rein, when the pony is allowed to take all the rein he wants and stretch his head and neck out and down as much as he likes, is an excellent reward for him when he has been working hard. Let him do it frequently when your are practising.

Leave the canter until last, because it is the most difficult pace to establish. Wait until you have established a fairly regular walk and

Active and well-balanced, the pony is happily taking the rein as it is offered to her by the rider, whose hands are very soft and relaxed.

trot. This means you have improved your sense of feel and rhythm, and your ability to apply your aids promptly and smoothly. It means that the pony's balance and responsiveness have improved so much that the canter will come more easily. At this pace the rhythm should be particularly well marked, the pony going forward boldly but without excitement, bringing his hind legs well under him.

Good paces are the basis of everything in riding, whatever you want to do with your pony. This is why so much importance is attached to them in the show ring and in dressage tests. They are equally important for jumpers, eventers, hunters and games ponies. They are essential in making a horse or pony a good 'ride', so that you can enjoy going out and about on him.

By the time you sit your C Certificate you should be able to ride your pony where you want at the pace you want — otherwise he will not really be under control. He should have a steady head, and bend the way he is going. Even if he is well trained and has a good temperament, you will have to practise and work on everything explained here. No pony will go well for a rider whose position makes life difficult or uncomfortable for him, or who has hard or unsteady hands and can't — or doesn't bother to — give clear aids. You owe it to your pony to learn to ride well enough to avoid causing him discomfort and confusion. You will find it is satisfying to spend some of your riding time trying to improve the way you go together.

5
OUT AND ABOUT WITH YOUR PONY: C CERTIFICATE

AS your position and ability to apply clear aids improve, and therefore your control over your pony, you will want to go further afield. This is good — it is very boring for both of you to spend all your time going round and round the same paddock. But there are certain things you must always remember when you go for rides, for the sake of safety, courtesy to others, and the well-being of your pony.

Always tell somebody, or leave a note, to say where you are going, and approximately how long you expect to be out, particularly if you are on your own. If you plan a long ride, it is safer and more fun to go in company.

Try to vary your rides as much as possible — it is better to make a round trip rather than go and return by the same route. Vary the pace, too. A good active walk is one of the best paces for getting your pony fit. Don't keep him 'at attention' all the time; let him have a long rein where it is safe to do so, so that he can really stretch out and use his head and neck.

The trot should always be steady, though still active — a fast, thumping trot is one of the worst things for a pony's legs and for his manners.

By all means have a canter in a suitable place, but do beware of bottles and hidden obstructions on grass verges.

Never let your pony get into the habit of going slowly away from home, then turning round and rushing back flat out — always make him walk the last kilometre, so that he arrives home cool and calm. Avoid always cantering in the same place. He will begin to anticipate and get excited as you approach that spot.

RIDING ON THE ROAD

The Ministry of Transport rules, from the Road Code, are set out below. They are simple and sensible, and you must obey them. It is best to keep off busy roads as much as you can.

Rules When Riding

Ride your horse on the left of the road, and as far to the left as is practicable.

Keep your horse on the grass verge or road margin whenever possible, but do not ride on a footpath, lawn or garden.

Do not ride more than two abreast.

Do not ride to the right of any moving vehicle, except when passing. When leading another animal, always keep it on your left (i.e. the animal on the lead must be farthest from the traffic.

Re-read the Do's and Don'ts on page 32. They still apply, no matter what stage of riding you have reached.

In town and city streets you must obey traffic signals and respect pedestrian crossings. The walk is the only safe pace in traffic. Ride in single file.

On country roads, use the grass verge, if there is one. If you have to ride on the metalled shoulder of the road — or on any metalled road — remember the danger of your pony bruising his foot on a sharp stone. Walk if the going is rough, especially if the pony is unshod.

In general. Learn the signals shown here and on page 67. Always warn other road users of your intentions. Always check the road is clear before moving off.

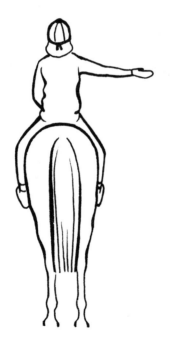

I intend to move out
or turn to my right

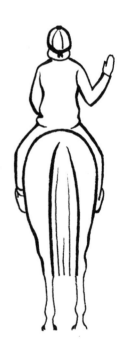

I am about to
slow down or stop

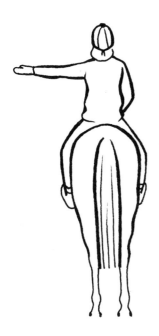

I intend to pull in or turn to my left

I am having difficulties controlling my horse please slow down

If your pony shies, turn his head *away* from what he is shying at. This is especially important if he shies at something on the side of the road. If you try to pull his head towards it, this could make him swing his hindquarters out into the traffic from behind. Use your right hand and right leg.

Never ride on the road after dark if you can possibly avoid it. If you do get caught out after dark, the following will all help to make you more visible: wear a white or light-coloured jersey or raincoat; tie a white rag or handkerchief round your right arm and another one on your stirrup iron; get some red reflective tape from a service station and stick it round the heel of your right boot, and, if possible, on your back.

Always be alert. Always show courtesy and consideration for others.

If your pony shies on the road, turn his head *away* from the cause. The grey pony's rider is using her right hand and leg correctly. The other pony is in considerable danger, and the rider is not helping by looking back.

RIDING ON FARM LAND

Never enter other people's property without permission. Find out exactly where you may go, and obtain permission, especially if you want to jump anything. Never jump when you are on your own. Don't ask to ride on farm land during lambing or calving seasons, after heavy rain, or if a farmer is obviously busy with shearing, etc.

Opening and shutting gates. Leave all gates as you find them. If somebody dismounts to open a gate, don't ride off until they have remounted.

If you dismount to go through a gate, always run the stirrups up, so that there is no danger of their getting caught up, and put the reins over the pony's head. Open the gate wide, and keep your hand on it as you lead the pony through. Look back to make sure he doesn't bump himself.

If you ride through a paddock with stock in it, cause as little disturbance as possible — walk, and go round the edge rather than through the middle. Never ride over crops, new grass or hay paddocks. If you cannot avoid going into these paddocks, keep to the fenceline.

Riding up and down hill. Start with gentle slopes. Try to keep the same pace, up, down or on the flat, first at the walk, then trot. Riding on rolling country is a splendid exercise for improving the balance of pony and rider, and for getting your pony fit before you start hunting or eventing. Lean slightly forward, up or down. On steeper hills, lean well forward and hold on to the mane or neckstrap going up. It is usually best to go straight down, unless there are definite cross-tracks which are wide enough for your pony to walk on. You should not go out on really steep country except in the company of an experienced person who can show you the ropes. Some ponies may need a breastplate and/or a crupper to prevent the saddle slipping in these circumstances (see page 184).

Be careful when crossing wooden farm bridges. They are usually slippery, so it is best to walk your pony across them.

If you have to tie your pony up on somebody's property, be specially careful to do it correctly — use a piece of baling twine, and tie to a post. If you tie him up in or around a yard, always borrow a shovel and clean up any droppings before leaving.

Opening and shutting a gate. The pony is parallel to the gate, with his tail towards the hinges. The rider uses the hand nearest to the gate.

Riding uphill. Hard work for the pony. On no account must the rider sit back on the pony's loins or interfere with his mouth.

Riding downhill. The pony is well controlled. Rider's position good, though a little stiff.

RIDING ON BEACHES

Make sure that riding is permitted. In some places ponies are allowed on beaches in winter but not during holiday periods. Always ride slowly among people who are walking, and especially among small children. Remember that dry sand is very heavy going and hard work for your pony.

Wading and swimming your pony are great fun, and very good for his legs, but you must find out about local conditions — quicksands, rips, currents and undertows — before venturing out. Go quietly, especially if any of the ponies are not used to water. Fast paces, noise and shouting could easily make them frightened or excited and difficult to manage.

Make sure your pony is well accustomed to wading before you think about swimming. It goes without saying that you must be a reasonable swimmer yourself, and that an experienced older person should be in the party. As salt water is bad for leather, it is best to take off the saddle. Always have a bridle on the pony to ensure proper control. Clean it well afterwards.

FORDING STREAMS AND RIVERS

Shallow streams with shingle bottoms are generally safe, provided you walk through them. Keep out of water if there are large stones or boulders, snags or branches in the water, or a swift current. Steeply-flowing rivers are often subject to flash floods, so beware of river crossings — even known fords — during or immediately after heavy rain, or if the water is so discoloured that you can't see the bottom. Water can be extremely dangerous, *always treat it with respect.*

RIDING ON RESERVES

Again, make sure that riding is permitted, and exactly where you may go. Keep off playing fields, new or mown grass or narrow footpaths.

RIDING IN FORESTS

This is permitted in some forest parks, and sometimes in private forest areas. There are two obvious dangers — fire, and getting lost. Don't strike matches or light fires. Make sure you know where you are going, and be especially sure to let somebody know you are going into the forest.

Have fun on your rides, but do remember that, unfortunately, not everybody likes ponies as much as you do. Some people are nervous of them. Whether you like them or not, there is no doubt that their hooves can do a lot of damage in a very short time, especially when the ground is wet. One or two thoughtless riders in a district can spoil the riding for themselves and everybody else.

Clean all your saddlery and your boots or shoes thoroughly the night before. Get up early so that you will have plenty of time to feed and groom your pony. There is no need to plait him up for a working rally, but his mane and tail must be clean and well brushed.

Dress

You *must* have a hard hat, with hat harness. If you are in your first year as a member, you will probably be allowed to ride in jeans, but you should get your Pony Club uniform as soon as possible: jodhpurs, white shirt, tie and jersey in your own club's colours. Everything must be clean and tidy, including your hair (use a hairnet, if necessary.) Wear your Pony Club badge, but no jewellery, which apart from being unsuitable, could be dangerous.

What To Take

Halter and rope, for tying your pony up. The halter may be put on over the bridle, with the rope tied round his neck. If the weather is at all doubtful, always take a raincoat or parka. For all-day rallies, you may need to take your lunch. If you have a long ride there and back, take a feed for your pony; it is easily carried in a strong plastic bag tied on to the saddle dees, or in a school haversack. In cold weather, especially if he is clipped, take a light cover for the pony — this can also be tied across the front of the saddle. Always take a hoof-pick and a small brush, to tidy your pony on arrival.

Leave in good time, so that you don't have to hurry. Allow for a speed of about 9kmh, and aim to arrive twenty to thirty minutes before the start of the rally. On arrival, dismount, run up stirrups, slacken girths. Offer the pony a drink, tie him up, give him a quick brush over and pick out his feet; then leave him to rest while you give any assistance you can in setting out jumps and other equipment.

Before your class starts, remove your pony's halter and cover, and put all your belongings tidily together in a safe place.

If you go to Pony Club by float, you must still do your best to get there early. In this case, you should ride your pony round quietly at walk and trot for ten to fifteen minutes before the start of your class, so that he will be settled down and ready for work.

At Pony Club you will spend some time working in a school or 'manege' on drill movements and various exercises in a ride. This teaches you to think quickly, and to apply your aids promptly but smoothly to maintain your place in the ride; it also gives variety and keeps everyone, ponies and riders alike, awake and alert. You learn to ride your pony accurately, and exactly where you want him to go, which is essential for success in games or jumping. If you can't do this at steady paces in an enclosed area, you won't have much hope of controlling him when you are travelling faster in the open.

TERMS AND EXPRESSIONS USED IN THE SCHOOL

The track. This is the outside edge of the school, just inside the rope, where you should normally ride. Also called the 'outside' track.

The inside track. This is about 1.5 metres in from the rope — where the inside rider would be, when riding in pairs.

Right rein — clockwise, left rein — anti-clockwise. On the right rein, your right hand is on the inside, on the left rein, your left hand.

Inside hand and leg, and the pony's inside legs, are ones on the inside of the school or circle, or of the pony's bend.

Changing the rein means changing direction, which can be done in a variety of ways. Remember that your whip should nearly always be in the inside hand, so change both the whip and the diagonal when you change the rein.

Going large means rejoining the outside track after a circle or other movement off the track.

Pace and distance. When working with others in a ride, it is essential that everybody keeps the same pace and maintains their distance from the person in front. This should normally be about 3 metres. If any other distance is necessary for a particular exercise, your instructor will tell you. Many school exercises cannot be done at all if the ride is not properly spaced, so, even though you may find it quite hard work, this is something you must really concentrate on.

Correcting distance. If you do lose your distance, correct it as soon as possible (and without waiting to be told) by cutting across or turning before you reach the end of the school, not by trotting or cantering to catch up. (If one person has to cut across like this, all those behind must do so too, otherwise the gap will only be transferred from one place to another.)

Dressing means keeping in line or in position during any movement. Dressing 'by the left' means that you glance to your left, and keep in line with the person to the far left of the line.

The leading file is the leader of the ride; it is an honour to be chosen for this position. You must be careful to keep an even pace, to ride good corners (if you cut them, everybody else will have to cut them,

73

too, to keep up), and to listen to the commands and obey them promptly and accurately.

When working in a school, there is always plenty to think about, even when it is not your turn to carry out any particular exercise — keeping distance, using your aids to keep your pony straight on the long sides and to bend him correctly on the corners. Every corner he does well is a good suppling exercise; every time he cuts one or bends the wrong way, he is getting stiffer and more into the habit of doing them badly. This will be very hard to put right later on.

SCHOOL EXERCISES

These are generally performed in one of three ways: in single file, or in succession, or in 'rides' or sections. Here are some examples; firstly, in single file:

The diagram shows three ways of changing the rein:

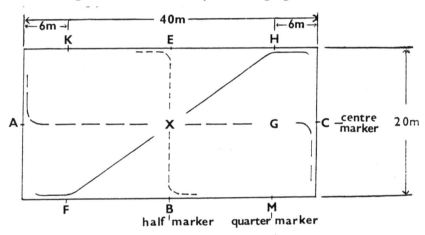

Three ways of changing the rein in the school: by inclining across from quarter-marker to quarter-marker, by turning down the centreline, by turning across the school.

A, by inclining across the school from quarter-marker to quarter-marker. You should leave the side when your shoulder (not the pony's) is level with the first marker. Go straight across and aim slightly to the inside of the second marker, so that your shoulder will come level with that one too. If you don't go to the markers the pony will fall in on the corners.

B, by turning down the centreline. The commonest faults are overshooting the first turn, through not preparing in time for the turn; or veering to the right before you turn left (or vice versa) at the other end. Straightness is all-important in this exercise.

74

C, by turning across the school. Once again, be sure to turn in time, and remember that in this case you have much less time to prepare for the second turn.

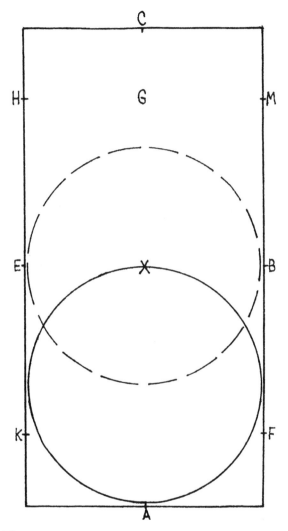

The large, or 20m, circle, at the end of the
school, in the centre of the school.

This diagram shows the large, or 20-metre circle which can be done either at the end or in the centre of the school. The former is easier, because you have three sides to help you. The main point about a circle is that it must be round, otherwise it won't achieve the object of bending the pony's body. Be careful not to go into the corners or to

75

flatten out on the sides when you are supposed to be on a circle, and think hard about applying your aids correctly.

It is most important in these single-file exercises that everybody, not just the leader, rides the movement accurately, and doesn't just allow their pony to drift round after the one in front.

The simplest form of individual exercise is trotting or cantering in succession from front to rear of the ride. One of the main things to remember is to start steadying in time, so that you don't shoot past or bump into the last pony, who might well respond by kicking you! Variations on this are to continue past the ride (out of kicking distance) and fit in behind when you catch up again with the rear of the ride. This makes you really use your legs to keep your pony going if he is inclined to be lazy .

Exercises In Rides

For example turns across the school in rides, with and without a change of rein. If the command is 'No 1 Ride, right turn,' everyone in No 1 Ride turns right at the same time, dresses by the right, and turns right again on the other side, without any further word of command. If the command is 'No 1 Ride, right turn and change,' you turn right as before, but dress by the left and turn left, again without any further word of command, on the far side. (It may sound complicated, but you will soon see how it works out in practice.)

These are just a few of the exercises that can be done in a school — you will learn many more as your knowledge and ability increase. It is a lovely sight to see a ride working alertly as a team, and you will gain much pleasure and satisfaction from being a part of it. You might like to develop some of these exercises into a musical ride which could be performed at your club gymkhana or an agricultural show.

BEHAVIOUR AT RALLIES

Always be punctual. Should you arrive late, apologise to your instructor and ask permission to join the class. Remember that Pony Club is a youth movement, not just a riding school; to get the most out of it, you must be prepared to give as well as take, and to take part in everything that goes on. During lessons and lectures, listen, watch and learn. If anything is not clear to you, ask. Be ready to help at all times. Attend to your pony's needs before your own, especially at lunchtime, when you should unsaddle, water and feed him.

Never forget to thank your instructor at the end of the rally. Help to put gear away, then ride home steadily. Walk the last kilometre.

It can be a long day for a pony, especially one who is not very fit.

Next day, check for soundness and injuries such as girth galls, brush him over and give him the day off.

CAMPS AND TREKS

These are two of the most enjoyable Pony Club activities — sometimes combined in the form of a trek over several days, with overnight camps. They both involve longer than usual hours of riding, so you and your pony must be fit if you are both to enjoy them to the full. To ensure this, exercise your pony regularly and give him some hard feed for at least a week beforehand. Check that his feet and shoes are in good order, and get him shod in good time if he needs it.

Check all saddlery thoroughly, too — in time to allow for any repairs. Make sure that the saddle is not coming down on the pony's withers, or pressing on any part of his spine. Get it restuffed if necessary.

Finally, go over the list of equipment you will be given, and see that you have every single item on it, and that everything is clearly marked with your name. You will not be popular if you have to go round borrowing from other people, or if you are always losing your belongings.

HUNTING

If your parents hunt they will tell you all about it and will take you out with them when they think you are ready to go. Otherwise, you should start with a children's hunt, where you will be taught about hunting procedure and etiquette. Some of the main points to remember are:
1. The Master is the most important person in the field — you must always obey his directions promptly.
2. The Hunt officials — the Master, Deputy Master, Huntsman and Whips — have right of way. Let them go first at spars or gateways. Hold gates open for them if necessary.
3. Never ride too close to hounds, so that you distract them or, worse still, are in danger of jumping on them. If hounds pass close to you, turn your pony's head towards them. To kick or injure a hound is unforgivable.
4. Respect the property you hunt over. If you open a gate, be sure you shut it, or that the people behind know that it must be shut. Don't jump unnecessary fences, and never attempt to jump a gate. If you do any damage, report it at once to the Deputy Master. The usual rules for riding on farm land apply when hunting.
5. Be quiet and keep still when hounds are drawing, or at a check. If

you rush about and make a noise, this will distract hounds and spoil the sport for everybody.

6. Keep at the back of the field until you have had some experience and are sure you can manage your pony if he gets excited among the others. If he refuses at a spar you *must* go to the back of the queue until everyone else has had a go.

7. Turn yourself and your pony out as smartly as you possibly can, and make sure that he is reasonably fit and in regular work. Take care of him in the field, and go home if he is tired.

8. Don't go out hunting until your instructor says you are ready. Some hunts do not allow people to go out, except to children's hunts, under the age of fourteen, so check on this.

Having approached the pole straight, the rider allows the pony to stretch down while she is looking up herself.

6
JUMPING: C CERTIFICATE

MOST PEOPLE enjoy jumping, and ponies enjoy it too — provided they have been properly trained and ridden, and haven't been sickened with too much of it. Jumping is a part of riding — you learn both at the same time. You can make a start on the jumping side as soon as you can walk, trot and canter, and can control your pony at these paces.

Some people seem to think that all you have to do to learn to jump is to stay on while your pony carries you over. This is of course quite wrong, and anybody who approaches jumping in this way is heading for trouble. As with everything else, you have to start at the beginning.

A lot depends on your pony. A steady, experienced pony will help you to learn quickly, whereas if he is young or excitable things will have to be taken much more slowly.

The main thing is to keep control, so that your pony doesn't develop bad habits while you are learning to present him correctly at the fence; and to maintain your position, so that he can jump freely and comfortably.

JUMPING AT HOME

Look at the pictures on page 87 for advice on jumping gear. If you are going to practise jumping at home you will need enough to build three jumps to begin with — six stands and about a dozen poles. Have a neckstrap on your pony, and always wear your helmet, with harness.

Start by laying one pole on the ground in the middle of a flat area of your paddock, so that you can approach it from either side, then walk your pony over this pole. Make sure that you get absolutely straight, at right angles to the pole, and right in the middle of it, and that you go straight afterwards as well as before.

Before you approach the pole, bend forward from the hips, just so that your shoulder is over your knee, but your seat is still in contact with the saddle; keep your head up, heels down, and lower leg in its normal position, close to the pony's side, ready to urge him on quietly if he should hesitate. Keep this forward position all the time.

As he steps over the pole, the pony will want to stretch his head and neck down to look at it. Try to let your hands follow forward and down, towards his mouth, just as much as he 'asks' you to, so that you keep a light contact, and therefore control, but he has all the freedom he needs.

When this is going well, do the same thing at a steady, rising trot, still remembering to keep your shoulders slightly forward. Circle left and right alternately, don't go the same way every time. There is no need to alter stirrups at this stage.

Now lay out about six poles on the ground, arranging them so that you can ride smoothly from one to the other without having to make any sharp twists or turns. The diagram shows a good, flowing layout.

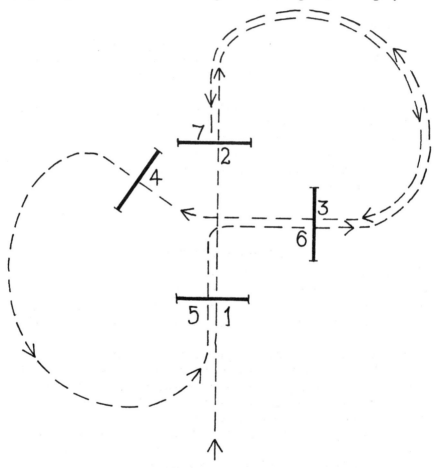

This simple layout allows for plenty of practice in riding straight and in making smooth turns.

Practise riding round this 'course', always getting straight before and afterwards, at right angles to the centre of each pole. To do this, you will *have* to look where you are going, and you will soon see that

80

it goes more smoothly if you remember to use your aids properly, to bend your pony so that he too looks where he is going, and keeps his even pace. You will find, when it comes to jumping, that the real fun of it is not going over and over one fence, but riding courses. You are now practising all the things that will help you then — looking where you are going, getting straight, keeping forward, keeping contact. Don't try to hurry this stage — keep on for a few days, or even a week or two, until you both get into the habit of doing these things correctly.

Now you will be ready to begin some actual jumping. Use just one obstacle to begin with; you could put it up against a fence line to help you keep straight. Put two poles together on the ground, with a stand at each end, and walk and trot over them in the usual way. Then put one end of each pole on the lowest peg, so that you have a little criss-cross about 30cm high. Trot at this, giving a slight nudge with your legs for each of the last three or four strides, and your pony should make a small jump over it, so remember to keep forward — shoulder, knee and toe in line. If you find you are inclined to lose your balance and come back, just slip your reins into one hand on the approach, and put the other hand forward on the pony's neck, or on the neckstrap. After he has landed, take the reins back into both hands.

A hand on the neck helps you to keep your balance. Neckstrap handy in emergency.

This helps you to stay forward in the right position, and after a few 'pops' like this, you should find that you can keep your reins in both hands and concentrate on feeling how much rein the pony 'asks' for, just as you did over the poles on the ground.

81

Next, put one pole straight across on the lowest pegs, and the other one on the ground underneath it, and pop over this in the same way. If you do this five or six times each time you ride, for a few days, it should become just as easy as riding over the poles on the ground. You may find it smoother if the pony canters the last few strides into the jump, but be sure to steady him back to the trot afterwards, and don't let him get into the habit of 'rushing' at his fences.

You can now begin to substitute small jumps (not more than 30cm high) for the poles on your 'course', and practise riding round it as you did before. Think of the same things: look where you're going, get straight, keep forward, keep contact. If at any time you get 'left behind' and lose your balance, grab your neckstrap quickly — *never* hold on by the reins. Put your hand on the neck again for the next few jumps until you get your balance back.

You should also begin to use your poles on the ground in a different way, as shown in the next diagram.

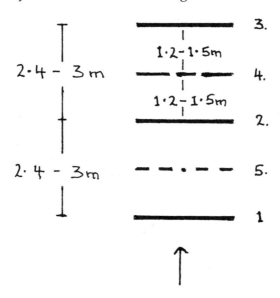

Trotting poles. The distance between them will vary according to the size of your pony, but it must always be even.

Start with three poles, first at walk, then at trot. The pony should keep his head and neck lowered as he goes over the three poles, and this will help to improve your 'feel'. When you can do these quite well, with the pony keeping a calm regular pace, you can begin to fill in the gaps; first the far one, between the second and third poles, then the nearer gap, so that you have a row of poles quite close together.

It is best to do these only at the trot, because they will not fit in with the pony's walking stride. It is most important that they *do* fit in with his trot stride, so that he goes over them smoothly, putting one foot in between each pole, and not being forced to put in a short step. You must measure the distance every time you use these poles, and be sure to get it right for your particular pony. If in doubt, ask your instructor when you go to Pony Club.

Cavalletti are another good exercise for both of you. You learn to keep your balance in harmony with the pony's movements, and to maintain a constant, steady contact with hand and leg, so that you can control his pace and direction all the time and he learns to go calmly over anything in front of him, without excitement or hesitation. You should find, as you practise together, that you both get the 'swing' of it — you really feel the pony rounding and swinging his back as he lowers his head and neck, and the one-two beat of his trot will be more marked as he steps over the poles. Rising trot will be easier for both of you.

This is quite hard work for your pony, so don't go on too long, and give him plenty of rests on a long rein.

Cavalletti. A useful follow-on from trotting poles, and an excellent way of learning to follow the movement of the pony's head and neck in jumping.

THE NEXT STEP

By this time, your control on the flat should be becoming more certain; the basics of jumping — balance, straightness, calmness, control — should be thoroughly established, and you will be ready for the next step. This will probably have taken about a month from the time you rode over your first pole on the ground — longer, if your pony is 'green' or excitable.

Length of stirrup. During the early stages of riding over poles and very tiny jumps, your stirrups were the same length as you had them on the flat — called 'general purpose' length. But during this time you should have been getting deeper in the saddle, and have let your leathers down a hole or two. This will make them too long for jumping, especially when you begin to tackle even slightly bigger fences, so your stirrups should now be shortened by one or two holes from your normal riding length.

If your stirrups are too short, your balance and ability to apply your leg aids will be affected; if they are too long, you will lose the bend in the knee essential for jumping, and your seat will be weak and unsteady.

A workmanlike pair. A firm jumping position and a well-balanced pony.

Jumping Position

Look at this picture of the jumping position. Shortening the stirrups has put the rider's seat further back in the saddle, but her weight is not on the pony's loins because she is leaning forward so that her shoulder is over her knee; to keep the straight line from elbow to bit when she brought her body forward, she has had to shorten her reins a little, and her hands are lower down than for riding on the flat, on either side of the pony's neck. Head up, heels down, lower leg in contact, as always. Spend some time practising this position at walk, trot and canter, until you can hold it steadily at all paces.

Now look at the pictures on pages 86 and 87, of the four phases of the jump — approach, take-off, flight and landing. Notice how the pony stretches out his head and neck a little on the approach, to look at the obstacle and size it up. As he takes off, he shortens his neck as he brings himself back on his hocks, so that he can raise his forelegs and push himself into the air. In flight, as he comes over the top of the fence, he stretches his neck right out to balance himself in landing, then shortens it once more as his forefeet touch the ground. The rider is sitting very close, almost completely still, conforming with supple back, hips, knees and ankles, to all these movements of the pony. She has maintained contact with hand and leg throughout, always looking ahead and in complete control of the situation. Notice how her hands follow forward and down towards the pony's mouth, not up towards his ears, in that moment of maximum stretch over the fence. This is most important.

Now go back to your one single jump, and put it up a hole, so that it is about 45 cm high. When you have done some trotting over poles and one or two smaller jumps to warm up, practise your jumping position over this one. Think very hard about those pictures, and get whoever is with you when you are jumping — for you must *never* jump by yourself — to tell you how you compare with them. It will take a lot of practice, but until you can keep your position consistently over 45-60cm you must not, in fairness to your pony, make the jumps any higher.

But this certainly doesn't mean that you should keep on jumping over and over the same fence — nothing could be more boring. Carry on with your practice over varied courses of jumps and trotting poles — the more you change them round the better. It will still be best, especially if your pony shows the slightest tendency to get excited, to trot between fences; you will have more control and find it easier to get straight.

A useful arrangement is 'three in a line', which is a good one for practising changes of direction and getting straight at each fence. Do this exercise first at trot, then at canter, and then alternate the pace, which keeps your pony very attentive and gives you more practice in transitions. In canter, if your pony goes on the wrong leg, do just what you would do in your normal riding on the flat — bring him back to trot or walk, circle towards the leg you want him to lead on, check bend and aids, and ask him again. Don't jump the next fence until he is cantering on the correct leg.

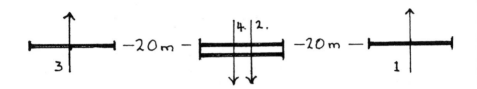

Three in a line.

Varying The Jumps

Try to vary the jumps themselves now. It is better, as your confidence and steadiness improve, to increase the width, rather than the height, and you can easily do this by putting another pole on the far or landing side. Keep your eyes open for suitable material for jumps — the pictures will give you some ideas. Always have a 'ground line' — something on the ground underneath or slightly in front of the fence. This helps the pony to sight it, as he judges his take-off by looking down at the ground. If he is in the least bit 'spooky' it is a good idea to introduce him to new things like drums or tyres by leaving a 'hole' in the middle, and gradually closing the gap as he gets used to them.

The four phases of the jump:
Approach, Take-off, Flight, Landing.

86

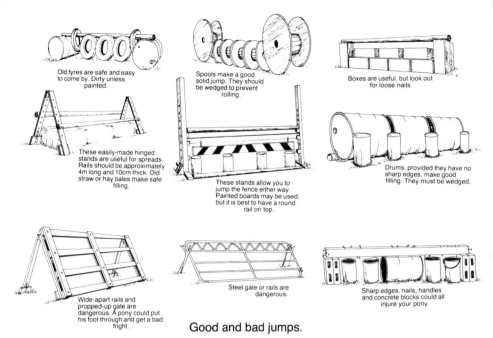

Old tyres are safe and easy to come by. Dirty unless painted.

Spools make a good solid jump. They should be wedged to prevent rolling.

Boxes are useful, but look out for loose nails.

These easily-made hinged stands are useful for spreads. Rails should be approximately 4m long and 10cm thick. Old straw or hay bales make safe filling.

These stands allow you to jump the fence either way. Painted boards may be used, but it is best to have a round rail on top.

Drums, provided they have no sharp edges, make good filling. They must be wedged.

Wide-apart rails and propped-up gate are dangerous. A pony could put his foot through and get a bad fright.

Steel gate or rails are dangerous.

Sharp edges, nails, handles and concrete blocks could all injure your pony.

Good and bad jumps.

A Simple Jumping Exercise

Start this exercise by putting a small jump after the poles — double the distance between the trotting poles from the last pole to the jump. This will help to regulate the pony's stride so that he meets the jump 'right', and it will encourage him to round his back nicely, so long as the distance is right for him.

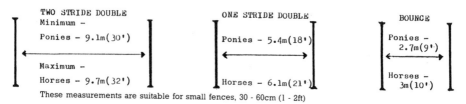

TWO STRIDE DOUBLE	ONE STRIDE DOUBLE	BOUNCE
Minimum –		
Ponies – 9.1m(30')	Ponies – 5.4m(18')	Ponies – 2.7m(9')
Maximum –		
Horses – 9.7m(32')	Horses – 6.1m(21')	Horses – 3m(10')

These measurements are suitable for small fences, 30 - 60cm (1 - 2ft)

NOTE Distances for doubles MUST be measured carefully to suit your pony or horse. Bad spacing can be dangerous. Ask your instructor for advice.

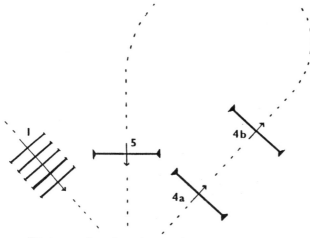

A good 'starter' fence

A good spread fence

A 'dropper' fills in the gap very well because –

The course shown here is a good one. There are several other useful tracks – how many can you find? All turns should be smooth, eg. from No 3 to No 2 is possible, but from No 5 to No 4 is not!

a single rail can be dangerous. Always use a dropper, more rails or filling

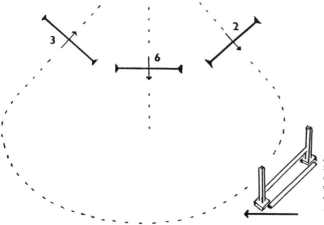

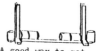

A good way to get your pony used to drums or other filling

A 'ground-line', just in front, makes the fence much easier for your pony, but unless you have one on the other side you can only jump the fence one way

Then add another jump, the same distance away — the pony should now go quietly over the trotting poles then straight in and out with a 'bounce' stride over the two little jumps, if you remember to keep him going with a steady lower leg — no flapping or kicking!

Jumping Without Reins

This is a wonderful way of working on your position, and especially good if your pony begins to jump less freely than he did, which could mean that he is not getting enough rein. Put your whip down, tie a knot in your reins, and start over a single, small jump. About 10 metres away — not at the last moment — drop your reins and put both hands forward on the pony's neck; keep them there until after he has landed and is going away from the jump. When this comes easily, do the same thing over a small in-and-out, seeing how still you can sit.

Now you can vary the proceedings by folding your arms, putting your hands on your knees or out to the side, making animal noises or singing a song as the pony jumps, clapping hands and counting 'one, two' as he pops over each one. All this helps you to relax and get your balance, and your pony will jump happily because he knows his mouth will not be interfered with.

Jumping without reins — flying angels!

If you have any particular problem in jumping — for instance, keeping your heels down or your head up, try saying 'heels' or 'head' out loud as you go over, and really concentrating on this part of your anatomy! You will probably be surprised at how quietly your pony will jump when you drop the reins. If he is a bit on the keen side, just let him canter the last couple of strides as you drop the reins, and jump going away from the gate or other ponies.

POINTS AND PRINCIPLES

To learn to jump, you need practice, but bear the following points in mind:

1. Jumping is fun for you but hard work for your pony, and the bigger the jumps, the harder he must work.

2. Always make sure that he is fit and well, that his saddle and bridle are well-fitting and comfortable, and that his legs, feet and shoes are in good order.

3. Variety is the spice of life! Vary the jumps themselves and their positions in the paddock. Sometimes work on your position and contact over trotting pole exercises or single fences, or in-and-outs, or on jumping without reins. At other times, concentrate on smooth riding from one fence to another, always making sure that the line between them is a flowing one, so that you *can* ride smoothly. Although calm, your pony must be alert and active, and these variations will keep him so.

When all these things are going well, and you have practised riding up and down hill without jumps, try putting your jumps on a gentle slope sometimes. Jumping uphill — get well forward to take the weight off the pony's loins — hold the mane or neckstrap if necessary. Jumping downhill — keep your heels well down, and don't get your shoulder in front of your knee. Small ditches and logs are excellent if you can find them, but *not* if you are on your own.

4. Little and often is much better than a long session occasionally. In the first six months of learning to jump, fences should not exceed 45-60cm, and it won't hurt to practise these two or three times a week, provided the ground is not very hard, and you don't go on too long. Fifteen minutes, or about ten jumps, allowing for rests in between, will be quite enough. After this, as you build up gradually to 60-75cm, cut it down to twice weekly at the most.

5. It is not a good practice to show your pony the jumps before going over them, and it should not be necessary if you go about it progressively, so that he gets the habit of going over anything first time.

6. Always finish on a good note. If he does one or two things particularly well, don't go on till he makes a mistake — stop there! Ride your pony forward with quiet determination, get straight and give him every chance. If you get left behind and hurt his mouth or back, give him a pat on the neck, and try not to let it happen again. If necessary, go back to something smaller, put your hand on the neck or use your neckstrap, or do some more jumping without reins. At the end of the session, reward your pony with a good pat or a titbit, dismount, run up stirrups, slacken girths and give him a few minutes complete rest. Don't forget to let your leathers down when you have finished jumping, and, of course, to tighten your girths before you remount.

If you have a good pony who tries to do what you ask and enjoys popping over small fences without getting too excited and if you tackle jumping in the way suggested here, you shouldn't have any problems. Just be sure that you can jump a variety of fences at one height before you raise them *at all*.

FAULTS AND PROBLEMS

Most problems come from lack of confidence or balance in pony or rider, and lack of systematic training. If things do go wrong, it's important to recognise and deal with the situation quickly and correctly, before it becomes a real problem.

Running Off To One Side Of The Fence

A rider problem! Causes: nearly always due to bad riding — not getting straight, reins too long, going too fast.

If it does happen, never let the pony complete his circle the way he wants to go. If he runs off to the left, pull your right rein quickly and firmly back towards the jump, then re-present him correctly. Don't go too far away — 10 to 15 metres is plenty. Once he realises you mean business and won't let him get away with it, he will soon behave.

Stopping Or 'Baulking'

It may occasionally happen that your pony will stop if he takes a sudden dislike to a new or unusual jump. If he does, hold him facing the jump for a moment, scold him and use your legs to let him know what you expect and then re-present him, pushing on more vigorously than usual. If he makes a bad or awkward jump, praise him for trying, but make him do it again until he does it properly, then dismount, big praise, finish. If he stops a second time, don't hesitate to lower the jump.

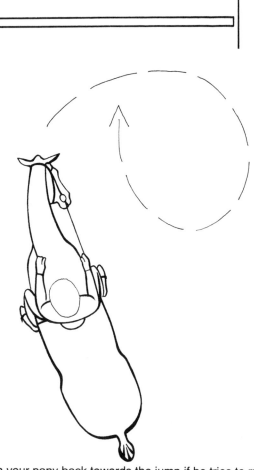

Always turn your pony back towards the jump if he tries to run off.

A lead from another pony, or even from a person on foot (not trying to pull the pony over, or even touching him, just hopping over in front) can be a tremendous help. Whatever happens, there must be no shouting or attempts to chase the pony over from behind. Never give in, but by all means lower the fence to ground level if necessary — the essential thing is to get him over.

If your pony begins to make a habit of stopping, you are heading for real trouble, and must do something about it at once. Possible causes:

Jumps Too Big and Too Much Jumping

A pony may be soured by too much jumping, and if the jumps are too big he may lose confidence. Answer obvious.

Rider Unsure

The pony takes his cue from you and, if you are unsure, he will quickly realise this and may lose his confidence. Don't be in a hurry to jump big fences — you have to lay the foundations before you can build a house.

Not Giving Enough Rein

This may come from the above causes. The pony must feel free to stretch over the fence, and some like to stretch more than others on the approach. If this is not allowed, they will often stop.

Loss Of Confidence

Due maybe to a fall, or to progressing too quickly. Can affect either pony or rider. Build up over smaller fences until you both feel happy again.

Discomfort

Often overlooked, but if, for no apparent reason, a pony who usually jumps well suddenly starts stopping, or jumping awkwardly or unwillingly, there *must* be a reason. Check carefully for: badly fitting saddle, pinching or pressing on the withers or spine, a sore back, girth galls, sore mouth, shoes left on too long, splints just forming or sore shins due to hard ground. All these can cause pain and put the pony off jumping, and of course it would be most unfair to try to force him to jump in such circumstances.

Excitement In Jumping

If your pony rushes off on landing, make sure that you are not giving him a hefty kick at the last moment, in front of the jump. He does not need to be told when to take off, and a last-minute kick will only make him rush off on landing.

On finishing a course of jumps, especially if the pony is excited, always circle him and make him walk or even halt, as soon as possible; then walk on a long rein. If returning to other ponies, always stop away from them, and walk back to your place.

If in doubt, stop jumping at home until you have been to Pony Club. Tell your instructor *exactly* what has been happening, and make sure you follow his or her advice to the letter.

7
COMPETITIONS

THIS BOOK has covered, so far, all the basic work on the riding side. You should now have a reasonable position and be able — provided your 'Care of Pony' is up to standard — to control your pony on the flat and over small fences. You should be able to attain your C Certificate — the minimum aim of every Pony Club member.

In addition, many of you are sure to want to enter for competitions. These vary from gymkhanas to horse trials. As well as being fun, they help to provide that extra incentive to improve yourself and your pony.

GENERAL CONSIDERATIONS FOR ANY COMPETITION

First, make sure, before entering, that it is suited to your standard of riding, and to your pony, that you have practised everything suggested for that type of competition, and that you are really ready for it. On no account enter if your instructor advises against it — there is plenty of time ahead of you.

Remember that it is most unlikely that you will win at the first attempt, and that nobody wins every time, so don't enter at all if you are not prepared to take the rough with the smooth. There is nothing worse than people bursting into tears when they are beaten in fair competition, or losing their tempers and taking it out on their ponies. The important thing is not winning, but taking part — that is where the fun and companionship come in. So do your best, both in training and on the day, and then take it as it comes. If you can make each occasion your 'personal best', you should be very happy, and you will be sure to be rewarded eventually!

Preparation Of Pony — Fitness And Training

Your pony must be in good condition, not too fat or too thin. He must be in reasonably regular work — ridden at least three times a week if you are entering for gymkhanas and local shows and sports meetings, five times if competing most weekends, especially in jumping or eventing (horse trials). Hard feed may be needed according to the time of year and the type of competition (see page 137).

Know The Rules

If they are not printed in the schedule, find out about them beforehand — ask your instructor, if in doubt. It really is disappointing to be eliminated on account of a rule you know nothing about — as, for instance, failing to go through the finish flags after you have jumped a clear round. Rules may sometimes seem complicated and unnecessary, but there is a good reason for them all. They do give everyone a fair chance, and it is up to you to learn them.

Pony Club gymkhana.

On The Day

Turnout: pony, saddlery and rider must be as near perfect as you can make them; remember you are representing your club or branch. Your pony must have been groomed and your tack cleaned regularly beforehand — don't rely on a last-minute clean-up. Everything that can shine, *should* shine. Saddlery must be sound and well-fitting; otherwise, if there is a gear inspection, you won't be allowed to start. Always check carefully what saddlery and equipment is permitted. Don't forget your Pony Club badge.

Always Be Punctual

You will be eliminated from almost any competition if you are not ready to enter the arena when your name or number is called, and you must give yourself time to saddle up and work in. You won't do your best if you have had a rush at the last moment.

Take Care Of Your Pony

Much depends on him, and you want to give him every chance to do his best. Don't use him as a mobile grandstand to watch what is going on, or gallop about on him between events. If you have only a short time in between, dismount, run up stirrups and slacken girths. If there is a longer interval, give him a drink, unsaddle him and tie him up to rest in a cool place, but out of draughts if the weather is hot, and keep him well covered if it is cold. You should give him a pick of grass or a small feed at some time during the day, but not just before an event.

Working-in

Essential for loosening up and getting the pony in the right mood. Time required varies according to the temperament, fitness and experience of the pony, and the type of competition. If he has had a long break during the day, he will need another, shorter, work-in period.

TYPES OF COMPETITION

Gymkhanas

Your local branch or club gymkhana or ribbon day will be the best place to make a start, because it consists largely of the games and races you already know from your Pony Club rallies.

Fitness and training. Even for a small local gymkhana your pony has got to be fairly fit. You will probably want to enter for at least four to six events, and with heats, semifinals and finals, this can be quite a hard day's work for him. If he is not in regular work, he will end up tired and sore, so you must make an effort to ride him at least every other day for about an hour, for several weeks beforehand. If he is too fat or too thin, if he sweats a great deal or feels sluggish and uninterested, he may need supplementary feeding (see page 129). He must be brushed over before work and thoroughly groomed afterwards, especially if he has been sweating.

Useful things to practise at home are:

1. Mounting and dismounting from either side. Vaulting on is invaluable for many games and gymkhana events, as well as being a wonderful agility exercise.
2. Riding and guiding your pony with the reins in one hand — and, of course, with your legs.
3. Getting your pony used to going up to all kinds of things — e.g.

buckets while you throw potatoes into them — without shying.

4. Stepping over poles, cavalletti, pegged-down polythene, etc.

5. Carrying such things as flags, handkerchiefs, sacks of straw representing dummies, etc.

6. Teaching your pony to lead in hand freely from either side at all times, even when you are going over 'stepping-stones' or hopping along in a sack.

When practising for such things as bending races, start at the walk, and only increase the pace gradually as the pony begins to understand what is wanted. In any case, a steady canter is quite fast enough — concentrate on skimming past the posts as closely as possible and making a neat turn at the end. Then, with the extra speed you are sure to get when competing against other ponies on the day, you should be well away.

Fifteen to twenty minutes practice on different things each time you ride will be plenty. Spend the rest of the time going for varied rides, including some work on slopes, if possible, mostly at walk and trot. This will give your pony the exercise he needs to build up his muscles and make him fitter.

On the day. Gymkhana events call for agility and quick reactions in pony and rider, but do try to keep calm — more haste, less speed is very, very true here! Do your best to avoid pulling your pony's mouth about or he won't enjoy his side of things very much, and may soon start to throw his head about and become difficult to manage. A good pony soon learns what is wanted for the various events, and he will be just as keen as you are to beat the other fellow.

Here are some of the other competitions that are often held at gymkhanas, shows and sports meetings:

Turnout Classes

Inspection at Pony Club should have given you a good idea of what is required for these events. The great thing to remember is that the judge wants to see *your* work in grooming and tack-cleaning, not your parents'. Saddlery must be correctly fitted and safe, as well as clean.

Best-rider Classes

The worst thing about best-rider classes is that everyone tries so hard to be still and 'correct' that they end up completely rigid, with no sense of 'feel' or harmony. You must try to look as though it is becoming quite easy and natural for you to keep that 'correct' position. On the flat, the way you apply your aids, the smoothness of transitions, the way the pony goes in all his paces (see page 62), and the partnership between you will all have a big influence on the result. In jumping, think of stillness over the fence, looking up, steady lower leg, hands following, smoothness and correct bend of pony between fences.

Best Pony Classes

These classes depend mainly on the conformation, or make and shape, of the pony. They are not held very often at Pony Club functions, because it is how your pony goes, not what he looks like, that really matters.

A show pony should be in fairly big condition — round and well-covered, not fat and flabby. He must, of course, be beautifully turned out, trimmed, groomed and plaited. The art of showing your pony is to have him going calmly but gaily whenever the judge's eye is upon him. If you watch the people who are successful in show classes, you will see that they always seem to manage to have their pony in a space, rather than shut in among all the others, and they achieve this without cutting across inside other competitors, so that they come between them and the judge. This would be very bad manners.

Best Paced And Mannered Pony

Here training is the main thing, and your good all-rounder should have as much chance as anyone else. Read 'Your Pony's Paces And The Way He Should Go' and also 'Training for Dressage Tests' (see pages 102-4). Smoothness in transitions and correct canter leads are most important. You may be asked to give an individual show. If the judge tells you what he wants you to do, listen carefully and do exactly that and nothing else. If it is left to you, remember that it is better to do simple things really well than try something more ambitious that doesn't quite come off.

Saddlery

For the last four classes, you should not have a martingale or a breastplate on your pony, or bandages or boots. The only sort of saddlecloth that should be used is a sheepskin. Until you have had quite a lot of experience it is best to use a snaffle bit, with or without a dropped noseband. Later on, you may wish to use a half-moon pelham (*not* a jointed one) or a double bridle, but ask your instructor's advice before doing this, and be sure to learn how to fit and use it correctly.

School Pony Classes

Two people 'double-banking' on one pony. Make sure that the pony is used to this before attempting it at a gymkhana, but remember that the 'pillion passenger' is sitting on the weakest part of the pony's back, and don't practise for too long at a time.

Obstacle Races

Almost 'anything goes' here, sometimes including small jumps.

JUMPING COMPETITIONS

These are basically of two kinds — round the ring, and F.E.I. (The initials stand for Fédération Équestre Internationale, the body that controls all riding and driving competitions at international level.)

Round the Ring

'Round the ring' jumping takes place over solid fences, which are set round the edge of the ring. It is judged entirely on style — you may be eliminated at the first refusal. This type of jumping is used for Pony Hunter classes at gymkhanas, shows and sports meetings, and for 'Best Rider over Hurdles' classes. The judges are looking for an even pace, not too fast, and a regular style of jumping, not taking off too close or too far away.

F.E.I.

In F.E.I. jumping the courses and fences are much more varied — at least one change of direction is always included in the simplest course. You are not marked on style, but there are penalties for refusals and for knocking down fences.

American Show Hunter Jumping uses a flowing F.E.I.-type course, with fences as natural as possible. It is judged under a set code, with no jump-off and strictly regulated heights. The emphasis is on style throughout the round.

Fitness And Training

You should start by entering the classes for your standard and age-group at your Pony Club gymkhana or ribbon day, where the size of fences is very carefully graded to give everyone a good chance of getting round. For this, 'gymkhana fitness', as described on page 94, will be enough, but if you want to do more jumping over bigger fences, your pony will have to be fitter than this. This means more feed and more exercise.

If you have practised on the lines suggested in 'Jumping' and have been used to going round varied 'courses' right from your pole-on-

Winning form, junior style.

the-ground days, finding your way round a novice Pony Club F.E.I. course should not be too difficult. The main thing is to be quite certain, from experience, that you can both jump any kind of fence you can think of, including doubles, up to the height you are likely to meet. It is most discouraging, and very bad training for your pony, to be eliminated at the first fence.

Don't think, just because you are going to enter for a competition, that you should do much more jumping at home — once or twice a week will be plenty. Some dressage training, to improve your pony's balance and make him more supple and obedient, will be invaluable, and of course he must have exercise as well as training.

On The Day

Walking the course on foot is essential for F.E.I. competitions, and you are always allowed to do this before you ride it. Walk the course *exactly* as you intend to ride it, and go round several times until you are quite sure not only which fence comes next, but also of the precise line you are going to take between each one. There will probably be a double, so make extra certain of your approach to this. Remember to walk through the start and finish flags — you will be eliminated if you forget them in the competition.

Before walking the course, you should have been riding your pony round for about half an hour to warm him up. Tie him up or get somebody to hold him while you walk the course, then get up again, check girths, and give him a few minutes steady canter work and two or three 'pops' over the practice fence. Don't keep jumping it over and over again.

In the ring. Make sure you are ready when your number is called. The starting signal is a bell — you have one minute to go through the start flags after the bell goes. Canter your pony on a circle close to the start flags — to the left if the first turn is left, right if it is right — so that he will be on the correct leg. It is very important that he should be settled, supple and attentive, so circle several times if necessary.

Then go through the flags and ride on firmly into the first fence, especially if it is away from the collecting ring and the other ponies. Keep calm, remember the line you worked out when you walked the course, try to maintain a steady, even canter, pushing on a little into each fence, and you will be surprised how easy and enjoyable it all is. After going through the finish flags, bring your pony back to the walk, give him a pat on the neck and a long rein, and leave the arena like that. It is bad manners and bad horsemanship to charge out flat-out at the end of your round.

If there have been several clear rounds (without any faults) there will be a jump-off over all or part of the course. The fences may be raised a little. If you have done your homework properly, there is no reason why you shouldn't be in the jump-off. If you are, make sure you know which fences you have to jump, and try to ride exactly as you did before — after all, it must have worked! Above all, keep calm and steady, even if the jump-off is against the clock. Jumping fast takes a lot of practice and training. If you try it too soon, you will probably knock fences down like ninepins, and will make your pony thoroughly excited and unmanageable into the bargain. The faster you go, the calmer you both have to be.

Check the rules especially carefully for F.E.I. jumping.

As round-the-ring courses are so much less complicated, there is no course-walking on foot for these classes, but you are usually allowed to ride round and show your pony the jumps. This should be quite unnecessary if your pony has been properly trained to go over anything in front of him, without expecting to examine it first; and it is not a good idea if you also want to compete in F.E.I. or Horse Trials, where the pony is never, in any circumstances, allowed to see the fences beforehand. Use the opportunity to take him into the ring and to check the line of the fences, without actually showing them to him.

In round-the-ring jumping there are no worries about finding your way round the course, but the sight of a line of fences straight ahead can be very exciting for a pony, so do guard against excessive speed, which would soon 'hot him up'. Always steady him and round him up on landing over each fence, so that he won't get faster and faster, the farther he goes. If you do much round-the-ring jumping, it is even more important to work your pony over trotting poles and jumping at different paces at home, so that you keep control.

JUNIOR RIDING TESTS AND DRESSAGE TESTS

'Dressage' means training, and this is what you have been doing all along, so it is really nothing new. Dressage or riding tests are performed in the same sort of arena that you ride in at Pony Club. They are designed to show how well you have trained your pony, and they include circles, turns, inclines, transitions — all the movements you have learned in your rides at Pony Club.

An example of a Pony Club Junior Riding Test is opposite page 1. Notice how it is divided into movements, for each of which you can get a maximum of 10 marks. The scale of marks shows just what each mark, from 0 to 10, stands for. It is not enough to walk, trot and canter on the correct leg where stated — if you don't do these things you may get 0 — 'not performed'.

But for good marks the judges want to see your pony going forward calmly but energetically, maintaining the rhythm of his pace through corners, circles or whatever movements are required, showing smooth transitions and changes of direction. He should have a steady head, should always bend the way he is going, and be attentive to your aids.

At the end of the test two very important marks, called the 'assessments', are given — one for the pony, smooth paces, correct bend, calmness and co-operation; and one for the rider, correct position, use of aids, control of pony. To get good marks for this last one you must have a reasonably good, steady position, and apply your aids smoothly and in plenty of time, so that the pony goes kindly and there is obviously a happy partnership between you both.

Fitness And Training

To do good dressage and carry himself as he should, a pony has got to be quite strong and muscular, so he must have regular exercise, apart from his training sessions, and enough of the right kind of food to make him feel fit and well, without making him too full of himself (see 'Feeding', page 128).

Re-read 'Riding: C Certificate', paying particular attention to all that is said there about position and aids, and to 'Your Pony's Paces And The Way He Should Go'.

When training, it helps to start with a good trot round in the open, to get your pony relaxed and supple. Use rising trot for this. Then work for a few minutes on yourself and your position. Practise sitting trot, both with and without stirrups, and the suppling exercises, to get deeper in the saddle. Try to get your stirrups a hole longer.

Next, think about the way the pony is going. Try to get his paces more even and to get him bending equally well in both directions. You must make him listen to you all the time he is working, and be sure to praise him when he does well, and to give him a rest on a long rein at frequent intervals. Work on transitions and remember to change direction regularly.

Practise transitions by riding beside a fence, and seeing if you can get the actual change of pace when your shoulder is level with one particular fence post. This will give you an idea of how long it takes you to bring your pony smoothly from one pace to another, and therefore how soon you must start preparing for a transition.

Halts will need practice too, to get them straight, still and attentive — in a working halt, the pony must be 'at attention', listening for orders and ready to obey them promptly. In all transitions, the correct order of the aids, and getting them working smoothly together, are most important. Remember to sit for the first or last few strides when going to or from trot.

A school at home. When all this work is beginning to show results you absolutely must put up a school at home (see the diagram in 'Out And About With Your Pony'). It is not fair to yourself, your pony, the judges or the organisers if you don't take the trouble to train properly for any event, and this is an essential part of training for dressage tests. Although you should be familiar with the movements from your work in the school at Pony Club, it is a very different matter when you go out there on your own to do a test.

The idea, in the school, is *not* to keep going through the test from beginning to end. If you do this, your pony will soon get to know it only too well, and will anticipate what comes next. Instead, practise the various movements of the test, or other movements of a similar standard, always in a different order, so that you keep him alert and listening for your aids.

Always enter the school by riding straight down the centreline to C. Ride round the outside track for a few minutes at walk and trot, thinking about corners and straightness on the long sides. If the pony does a bad corner — falling in or bending to the outside — circle round, check your aids, and go through that same corner again, and do this with any movement that is badly done.

Practise accurate changes of rein across the diagonal, down the centre or by turning across the school, and work on 20-metre circles, which are a prominent feature of nearly all Pony Club dressage tests (See diagram on page 75 in 'Out And About With Your Pony').

You will find it is helpful to mark X in the centre of the school (sawdust does well for this) and to put a marker exactly halfway between B and E and the corner — you could use coloured insulating tape wound round the rope. This will give you useful landmarks. When circling at the end of the school, you touch the sides at these points and pass through X; if the circle starts at B or E, you cross the centre line opposite these markers.

Don't canter in the school until your pony is reasonably well bent and balanced at the trot, and is cantering calmly in the open. Always ask him to strike off in a corner or on a 20-metre circle, not on the long side, which would make it more difficult to get him on the correct leg. He will have to take the corners quite a bit wider at first at the canter.

Junior riding tests. A good change rein, with the pony well placed for the corner.

Every dressage test begins by entering at A at the walk or trot and riding straight down the centre line to X or G, where you halt and salute the judges. This is another thing that needs practice, so that

104

your pony gets the habit of doing a proper 'working halt' every time. Girls salute by putting both reins into the left hand, right arm down to the side, and bowing the head. Boys may either salute this way, or by doffing the cap. Practise saluting, and always make your pony stand still afterwards for a moment, before moving off.

Although it is essential to practise in the school, don't go on for too long at one time. Always warm your pony up for five or ten minutes in the open, while you check your position, then work for about another ten minutes in the school — less, if he goes really well. If work in the school is overdone, it is very easy for a pony to become bored.

Before the competition, you should ride the test right through once or twice to get the feel and flow of it, but this will be quite enough.

On The Day

The right amount of working-in for your particular pony is most important, and this is something you only learn from experience. The first time, aim to be mounted about half an hour before your starting time, and spend the first part walking on a long rein, letting him settle down and get used to the surroundings. Then take up your reins, and work him in as you would before going into the school for practice at home.

When the previous competitor comes out, you are allowed to ride round the outside of the arena to let your pony look at the markers, the judges' cars, or anything else that might make him shy. Be sure you know what the starting signal is — it is usually a bell, but can be a whistle or car horn. When it goes, you have one minute to enter the arena, so make your way to A, do a circle outside the arena to get your pony's attention and to line up, then enter down the centre line, as you have practised at home.

In most tests, except at championship or area trials level, you are allowed to have a 'commander' to tell you what comes next. It is really much better to learn the test so thoroughly that you don't need this, because you have to know the next movement so that you can prepare for it in time. (The best way to learn the test is by going through it on foot in a miniature arena. You can 'walk, trot and canter' in the right places!)

While thinking ahead, try to keep a constant check on your pony's rhythm and bend and adjust your aids quickly to correct anything that needs it. Look as though you are enjoying yourself, and, above all, don't hurry.

Course errors. If the bell rings during your test, it indicates that you have made a mistake. Go to C, where the judge will tell you where to pick up the test.

Use of voice. You will be penalised if you use your voice during a test.

Collecting mark sheets. Always do this, and read them carefully, especially if you got low marks. The remarks will tell you what went wrong, and give you an idea of how to improve next time. If anything is not clear to you, judges will always explain if you go to them with your papers, so don't hesitate to ask.

Saddlery. Only a plain snaffle bit is allowed for dressage tests at Pony Club level (see Saddlery and Equipment, page 178). A cavesson, dropped or crossed (grakle) noseband may be used. Martingales, bandages and boots are all forbidden. A whip may be carried in all tests except at area trials and championships, but spurs are not allowed in junior tests.

Requirements at junior level

All that is expected in the junior riding tests is that your pony should maintain even paces, show some bend in the direction he is going, and have a steady head. By going willingly and calmly, he will show that he is accepting your aids, even though he may look (and feel) a little 'long' or unbalanced.

WORKING PACES

For dressage tests, working trot and canter and medium walk are required. In these paces, the pony should show more energy without going faster. As he uses his hocks more, his hind legs will take more weight and his forehand become lighter — rather like a seesaw.

As his balance improves, it will be easier for him to respond to your aids. You will get a feeling of lightness in the springiness of his movement and the way he carries himself. His head and neck will be a little higher, he will flex at the poll and relax his jaw. All this does not happen at once — the important thing to remember is that it must start with the pony bringing his hind legs further under him. It is *not* a question of using curb bits or other gadgets to pull his head in.

When training, still begin with the work in the open on a long rein. First get the pony walking actively, then have a good long trot (about five or ten minutes) always using rising trot until he has had time to warm up and get into the swing of his work. Take up the reins gradually until you have a light, even contact on his mouth. Now bring in circles and changes of direction, doing some of them in sitting trot, concentrating on keeping the rhythm — watch that you don't slow down when you sit and go faster as you start to rise again.

Then go on to transitions — only simple ones, from one pace to the next, but including canter if the pony is going calmly and you feel he is ready for it.

This is the basic pattern of work, but it will vary according to the pony's temperament. If he is lazy, he will need waking up, if nervous and excitable, he will probably need a much longer period on a long rein at the beginning, to get him relaxed and calm (see 'Problem Ponies', page 112).

But whatever his temperament, you should by now, after a suitable work-in period, be able to get your pony going attentively and accepting a steady contact with both hand and leg. Now you need the extra activity and lightness for those working paces. To get this, push up a little harder with your legs, but don't allow the pony to go faster — instead, when he tries to increase the pace, close your hands and 'ask' softly with your fingers. The pony should respond by bringing his hocks more under him, rounding and swinging his back and relaxing his lower jaw — he should feel shorter, lighter, springier.

This will need a lot of 'feel' on your part — if you don't stop 'asking' the moment he gives, he may throw his head up, become 'overbent' (with his chin tucked in to his chest) or drop behind the bit, so that the forward movement is lost.

You will probably get this feeling of lightness for only a stride or two at first. It is something that has to be developed gradually, because it means that the pony is using his muscles in a slightly different way, and he will find it *very* hard work at first. If he manages to hold it for five or six strides, praise him with your voice while he is actually doing what you want, then give him a long rein and a good pat on the neck.

When he is going correctly, bringing his hocks well under him with a softly rounded back and relaxed jaw, he is said to be 'on the bit', and he will be well on the way to working paces. You will certainly notice a big improvement in his responsiveness, and you will find that you can ride all your school movements more accurately.

In training, when things go wrong, ask yourself 'Why?' — 'How can I improve it?' 'Were my aids clear?' 'Does the pony understand what's wanted?' All training is repetition, but it is no use repeating the same mistakes over and over again. You must try to work it out, being absolutely honest as to whether it was your fault or the pony's. You can't expect everything at once — when you feel your pony has tried hard and shown some improvement, reward him and change to something else.

Give yourself plenty of time to prepare for a test, gradually stretching your practice time to twenty to thirty minutes overall, several times a week. Take less time than this if things go particularly well; or, if they go badly, and either one of you is just not in the mood that day. The great thing is always to finish on a good note if you possibly can. Vary this work with plenty of interesting rides, plus jumping and games practice.

Don't try to 'pressure-cook' yourself and your pony into producing a startling performance for one occasion, but think of improving your riding, the pony's whole way of going, and the partnership between you. You should find it a worthwhile challenge if you approach it in the right spirit, and you will certainly find the accurate control you will gain over your pony will stand you in good stead for anything else you want to do with him.

HORSE TRIALS

A horse trial, or one-day event, consists of three phases — a dressage test, which always comes first, followed by a cross-country round and then showjumping over F.E.I. fences. Occasionally the two jumping phases may be reversed.

Fitness And Training

Even a novice Pony Club horse trial demands quite a high degree of fitness in the pony — and the rider. If you doubt this, try running round the cross-country course on your feet, and remember that when your pony does it he will be carrying you on his back. And also that he will have to do the showjumping shortly afterwards.

In talking about fitness for other competitions, we have mentioned the three factors of feeding, exercise and grooming. All three are even more important for 'eventing'. Your pony must be ridden five or six times a week for at least a month before a one-day event, and this must include exercise as well as work, or training. Exercise is going for rides, mostly at a walk or steady trot, but certainly including the occasional canter for variation. Some steady road work helps to harden the pony's legs, and 'ups and downs' are wonderful for muscling him up and clearing his wind, so that he won't get too tired or 'blown' on the cross-country. About an hour a day of work and exercise combined will do for novice events, provided it is regular. For feeding and grooming, and also clipping, which may be needed during the winter months, see pages 128, 145 and 149.

We have already talked about training for dressage tests and for showjumping so we will deal here with cross-country. For the most junior Pony Club events — and please do start at the bottom! — the height of fences will not exceed 45-60cm, so it is not the size but the different types of obstacles you will have to think about. Do make sure that you are used to cantering — not just walking and trotting — up and down on rolling country, not on steep slopes. When you can maintain a steady even pace up, down or on the flat, try to maintain that same pace over small jumps on slopes.

You simply must practise over ditches, even if you have to manufacture a small one! Many ponies who can jump quite big fences will stop at the smallest ditch if they are not used to them, and there are very few cross-country courses that don't include at least one ditch.

Jumping obstacles in fence lines may be another thing that is new to your pony. If, up to now, he has regarded fences as things to keep him in, he may be quite startled at being asked to jump out over them! If it is possible to make a very small spar in a fence-line you would find this most useful. Most Pony Clubs have some cross-country practice fences, and you will have an opportunity to have a 'school' over them before you enter your first one-day event.

Ponies vary in the amount and type of training that they need, but, as a guide, try doing dressage work three to five times a week, trotting poles or cavalletti and jumping exercises once or twice, and either a showjumping or a short cross-country round once a week. If your pony is inclined to be excitable about jumping, you may find that it does him good to do trotting poles and one or two small jumps almost every day, to show him that this is just part of his normal work. It is really better to work him first and then take him out for exercise when he has 'finished on a good note', so that he ends up cool, calm and relaxed. Try to do it this way round if you can. Give him one day off a week, and on the following day give him a good long exercise session.

On The Day

Work-in and ride the dressage test as already described. It is important to know the time of your test, so that you can decide whether to walk the cross-country before or afterwards.

Try *to walk it at least twice*, so that you can plan exactly where and at what pace you are going to jump each fence. There may be several possible ways of tackling a particular jump, but you must know just how *you* intend to do it, and stick to your plan. It is usually best to take the easiest alternative if you are inexperienced, even if it means covering a little more distance. Thorough course-walking is more than half the battle for cross-country. Walk the showjumping course, too, during the morning, if you have time.

As your pony has already done his dressage test, he will probably need less working-in than usual for jumping. Aim to be mounted about twenty minutes before your starting time for the cross-country. Trot and canter round for a few minutes, and have two or three (not more) jumps over the practice fence. Remember to show yourself to the gear inspector before starting. Check your girths.

Riding the cross-country. Think ahead, and remember the plan that you worked out so carefully. Don't worry about speed. If you trot round the course you will get time faults, but if you keep a steady canter and take the shortest reasonable route, there should be no problems in a novice event. If necessary, you can speed up a little later on, as you gain experience. Try to maintain the forward position (shoulder, knee and toe in line) all the way, from start to finish. Head up, heels down (especially over drops). Keep well forward to take the weight off the pony's loins when cantering or jumping uphill. Sit as still as you can, keep a steady contact with hand and leg, and push on quietly for the last few strides into each fence. Have a good ride and enjoy yourself!

On finishing, pull up slowly, dismount, run up stirrups, slacken girths and turn your pony's head to the wind if he is blowing. Then lead him round for a few minutes until he cools off, but be sure he doesn't get chilled; throw a cover, or two if it is very cold, over the top of the saddle. If the pony is not kept warm, he will stiffen up and not be able to do his best in the showjumping.

Showjumping. This takes place over an ordinary F.E.I. course, and you should have done a few of these before entering for a horse trial. Some ponies may be more excitable than usual after the cross-country. If your pony is one of these, do some circles and transitions, especially working halts, and jump the practice fence several times at the trot until he settles down. It is most important in this case to keep a steady, even pace throughout the course — try to 'round the pony up' and not let him rush off on landing over his fences.

Of course you can do it!

8
PROBLEM PONIES

IT CANNOT be emphasised too strongly that problem ponies are only for experienced riders — and even they can't always get them right. A first or second pony must not, at the time you buy him, show any tendency to rear, kick, pull, buck or be nervous in traffic. He must be easy to catch and quiet to handle.

However, faults and problems always start somewhere, and while you are learning they may show signs of developing, even with your well-trained pony. The object of these notes is to help you recognise the start and possible causes of any troubles that may occur, and to take the right steps to deal with them before they become real problems.

UNSTEADY HEAD

Possible causes:

Hands Too High, Unsteady, Rough, Hard

Answer: obvious.

Unsuitable Or Ill-fitting Bit

Answer: try a thicker, milder bit, possibly a half-moon snaffle. Make sure it is the right size and fitted correctly.

Sore Tongue, Lips, Or Bars Of The Mouth

Check these very carefully if the pony *suddenly* starts to throw his head about. Treat injuries, and rest until healed. The injuries can, of course, stem from either of the two previous causes.

Teeth

Sharp molars can sometimes cause trouble. If no other obvious cause can be found, they should be checked (see page 163).

Nervous Or Excitable Temperament

Important to school calmly — see advice for 'Pulling', below. *Note:* too much racing about and jumping at fast paces can excite any pony, and once the tearaway habit is formed, it is extremely difficult to overcome.

PULLING

Possible causes: as above — also lack of work, spring grass, too many oats.

What to do. Check hands, bit, mouth, teeth. A dropped noseband may help if the pony evades the bit by opening his mouth wide or crossing his jaws. Give regular work, check feeding. Shut up part-time if spring grass is very rich.

In both these cases — if the pony's head becomes unsteady or he starts to pull or be less responsive to the rein aids long-rein work is most important.

Start by walking the pony on a circle, 20-30 metres in diameter. When he is going quietly, offer him a little more rein; not too much, at first, so that you can check him quickly but gently, without snatches, if he tries to go faster or break into a trot. He will soon understand that he can have all the rein he wants so long as he keeps his pace even, and then you can gradually give him more rein until he is on a 'long' rein, and enlarge the circle until you are riding round the paddock. Your voice will help a lot — a quiet, firm 'No,' when he is wrong, 'Good boy,' when he is right; stroke, rather than pat, his neck when you praise him — it has a more calming effect. Remember, all this probably started from misunderstanding and unintentionally hurting his mouth, so he is likely to be a bit nervous.

When the pony walks well on a long rein, try to get him to do the same thing at the trot; go about it in just the same way — starting on the circle, and returning to it if he gets excited when you go large round the paddock. When he is more settled in the paddock, it may be a good idea to take him out for long, steady rides for a few days, with plenty of walking on a long rein.

If the bit fits correctly and the pony normally goes well in it, it should not be necessary to make a change. If you really feel a more severe bit could be needed, do consult your instructor first, and regard the change as only a temporary measure until you have corrected the faults that caused the trouble.

LAZINESS

Could lead to nappiness — see below. Possible causes:

Poor Condition

Too fat, too thin, mineral deficiency, incorrect feeding. Worms and/or bots.

Pony too old or too young for the work demanded of him.

What to do. Check the pony's feeding, and check for worms. If too fat, shut up part-time. A little hard feed may help. If three years old or under, turn him out for several months to let him grow and develop, feed him well.

Boredom

Causes: (a) Lack of variety in riding, always doing the same thing, going the same way. (b) Lazy and unresponsive rider, not making the pony obey the aids, treating him as a machine.

What to do. (a) Try to vary the pony's work, take him to different places, work him in company if possible. (b) Check your aids to make sure you are giving them correctly. Work on transitions, using your whip if he ignores your leg. Keep him up to the mark and praise him when he does well. Don't keep on and on with any one thing so that he gets fed up with it.

If none of these measures brings about an improvement, and a normally active pony remains lazy and listless, have a veterinary check-up — there *must* be something wrong.

STUBBORNNESS OR NAPPINESS

Pony refusing to go forward at the required pace or direction, or unwilling to leave the gate or other ponies, but only too anxious to return to them. Possible causes: lazy, weak or undecided rider, unclear aids, ill-fitting saddlery.

Allowing the pony to go slowly away from the gate, then turn round and rush back to it.

What to do. If the pony persistently refuses to go forward at the pace you want, or insists on trying to take you where you don't want to go, it may be necessary to use your whip for punishment. Face him the way you want to go, then put your reins in one hand, turn your whip up the other way, as shown, and hit him hard and quickly, as close to your leg as possible, two or three times. Let him go forward at once.

If he is trying to go to the left, you *must* use the whip in your left hand — to hit him on the right side would only encourage him to go away from the whip, and he must on no account be allowed to turn left. If he is very determined, you may find it best to keep your reins in both hands — use a wide open right rein, but don't take your left hand up his neck so that he can turn his head too much; use both legs, the left one further back and more strongly, and growl at him.

Whatever happens, the more you have to punish him, the more you must praise him when he finally does what you want — even to the extent of giving him a titbit.

Just think: if he was a good, obedient pony when you got him, you must have brought a lot of this on yourself. At the same time, he mustn't be allowed to get away with it, because, apart from being quite serious in itself, this sort of thing can easily lead to rearing, one of the most dangerous vices of all.

REARING

As mentioned above, this can develop only too easily from nappiness, particularly if the rider uses the legs while at the same time unintentionally hanging on to the reins, so that the pony *cannot* go forward. A badly-fitting, uncomfortable saddle or too severe a bit are other possible causes.

What to do. If your pony really starts standing right up on his hind legs, you must get experienced help as soon as possible. It is more likely that he will give a series of 'bounces' with his forelegs a little way off the ground. The great thing is *not* to pull on the reins, which would probably make him go right up and could easily pull him over backwards, but to lean forward, leaving the reins completely loose, and drive him forward with your legs and whip as strongly as you can. Remember, he can't possibly rear unless he stops, so if you can teach him to obey your leg and keep moving, you will overcome the problem.

If your pony is nappy, use the whip on the side nearest to the other ponies.

BUCKING

Possible causes:

Sore back, ill-fitting saddle, pressing on wither or spine, broken tree, crupper ring pressing on spine.

Girth galls, actual or potential. Girth too hard, too tight or too loose, allowing saddle to slip forward or back.

'Cold back', especially if the pony has been clipped 'right out' and is not used to this.

Lack of work, spring grass, too many oats.

What to do: Check saddle, girth and pony's back and girth, and *take necessary action*. If due to cold back, use a sheepskin under the saddle, and be specially careful not to girth up tightly when the saddle is first put on. Lead him round for a few minutes before mounting. Any pony may give a little buck or 'pig root' if he is fresh and feeling well and happy. Sit tight, try to keep his head up and drive him forward, and take as little notice as possible! The more fuss you make, the more fun he gets out of it. Give him a good long trot to settle him down.

A simple method of stopping a pony from putting his head right down to buck or graze. He must be able to put his nose down to the level of his knees.

116

If bucking becomes persistent, use a strap or cord from the bit ring on one side across the wither to the saddle dee on the other side, as shown. This must be long enough to let him get his nose down to the level of his knees, but no further — which he will want to do if he is going to get a really good buck in. Change sides daily. This check-cord is also useful for ponies who persist in putting their heads down to graze. You should never allow a pony to graze when he is being ridden.

KICKING

Possible causes:

Other people riding too close and treading on the pony's heels and making him nervous.

Excitement in company, particularly if unaccustomed.

Bad temper, especially when mares are in season.

What to do. If the pony has good reason to kick, scold him (and the person who trod on his heels!) but don't punish him severely. If the excuse is insufficient, he *must* be punished. Use your whip, as for the nappy pony. While the pony shows any tendency to kick, it is up to *you* to warn others, and keep his head, not his heels, towards them. A red ribbon on the tail is the badge of a kicker, but you are responsible for him.

UNSTEADY OR DIFFICULT TO MOUNT

Possible causes:

Not always insisting that the pony stands still — not taking up the reins with sufficient contact to make him do this.

Poking him with the toe, or pulling on the reins or cantle of the saddle as you mount.

What to do. Check the above, and correct as necessary. If he is very tall, mount from a block or let the stirrup down.

TRAFFIC-SHY

It is most unlikely that your pony will become traffic-shy if he was all right when you bought him, unless he has been involved in an accident or there is some other obvious cause.

What to do. It may be possible to restore his confidence by taking him out — on a leading rein at first, if necessary — with a quiet, traffic-proof horse or pony between the nervous one and the traffic, or by keeping him in a paddock beside a busy road for a while. Whatever you do, on no account take him out on the road by yourself until you are really sure he has got over his fear. If he does not get over it, there are, unfortunately, only two alternatives if you have to ride on the road — *always* go out in company; or get another pony.

PUNISHMENT

Before you punish your pony, you must be sure of two things — that he understands what you want, and that he is capable of doing it. If there is any doubt in your mind, check your aids and try to make it clearer or easier for him. Notice how often the foregoing problems stem from bad riding — especially hard or unsteady hands and unclear aids; poor judgment — particularly too much galloping about, most of all on the way home or going towards the gate; uncomfortable, unsuitable or ill-fitting saddlery; or a pony who is not feeling well, possibly due to worms or inadequate feeding, or alternatively is feeling too full of himself owing to too little work and too much feed. All these points must be thoroughly checked before you accuse your pony of being 'stubborn'.

However, there are times when ponies, like people, are just plain naughty and don't want to do as they are told. If your pony's behaviour is defiant or dangerous, if he is nappy or kicks without grave provocation, he *must* be corrected. Partnership is most important, but you must be the senior partner — even a small pony is too big and strong to be allowed to take over the position of boss.

The pony must have confidence in you, but he must also respect you, otherwise you will soon be in trouble. If you are too weak, scared or sentimental to punish him when he honestly deserves it, eventually somebody stronger and more determined will have to do it, but by that time he may be well on the way to becoming a problem pony.

There are three ways in which you can punish a pony:
1. Voice. A deep, quick growl, not a lot of excited shouting.
2. Legs. Used more vigorously than usual, but *not* with spurs.
3. Whip. Always on the pony's ribs, as close behind your leg as possible, and only when the other two have failed. Nobody likes the idea of hitting a pony they are fond of, but the right type of whip, correctly used, will only produce a momentary sharp sting, which will be quite enough to convince him that you mean business.

The things you must never do are:
1. **Never** Punish a pony by deliberately jerking, tugging or sawing at his mouth.
2. **Never** Hit him about the head.
3. **Never** Get off and hit or kick him from the ground.

Treatment of this kind is abuse, not punishment, and shows a complete lack of self-control, unworthy of any Pony Club member.

If you do have to punish your pony, it is even more important to 'finish on a good note' and on good terms with one another. If these unhappy occasions are occurring rather frequently, look very hard at yourself! Remember that Pony Club is there to help you, so ask your instructor to advise you at the next rally.

YOUNG PONIES

Most problems with young ponies arise from inexperienced riders. It is foolish for a young or novice rider to buy a young pony and think that it is simply a matter of going quietly for a while and all will be well. In order to teach, you must have knowledge; the idea that you can learn together is nonsense. To try to learn on an untrained pony is unfair to both parties. The pony will become confused and is almost sure to develop some naughty, possibly dangerous, habits. You will get cross because he won't do what you want, and you may get a nasty scare into the bargain.

You must learn your aids thoroughly, and also a little of how a pony thinks and reacts, before taking on the job of schooling young ponies.

One of the problems is that a pony of two or three years old is usually *very* quiet, almost dopey, and this makes people think they have found the answer — a quiet, cheap pony. Wait until he is four or five, when it is more than likely he will suddenly wake up with a repertoire of tricks that will take some sorting out!

So leave young ponies to more experienced riders.

Ponies should be three years old before they are broken in to ride — even then, they should only be lightly ridden, and they should not start jumping until they are nearing four years. This is because ponies grow until they are five or six, and their bones are quite soft in their early years. Their size, and the fact that they are such willing creatures, lulls people into thinking that they can start work after only one year in the nursery. This ruins many good ponies and horses. Their backs, legs and joints suffer, and they become sullen and lifeless — broken, in every sense of the word.

Properly handled, and given time to grow up physically and mentally, a pony should be in his prime by eight years, and continue to enjoy life and provide enjoyment until he is at least eighteen.

Whatever your experience, if you have a young pony, be sure to ask advice on any problems as they arise. It is better to sort things out quickly than to wait until bad habits are established. Don't expect the pony to jump beyond what is suitable for his age and experience, even if you feel he is capable. In short, follow your instructor's advice in every way — if you are patient, there will be plenty of good times ahead.

119

PART III

CARE OF THE PONY

9

PADDOCKING: C CERTIFICATE

REQUIREMENTS OF A PONY AT GRASS

PRACTICALLY all ponies in a temperate climate live out in a paddock — at grass. This is the nearest thing to their natural way of life but, of course, they are not free to wander where they will in search of food and water, as they do in the wild state. It therefore becomes your responsibility to see that their few essential needs are supplied. It is a small return for the pleasure and companionship you get from a well and happy pony.

These are the things your pony needs:

1. An unlimited supply of clean, fresh water.
2. Sufficient good pasture, with supplementary feed of hay or hard feed (see page 129) when grass is short, or when the pony is working hard.
3. A safe paddock, with good fences and gates, and free from weeds and poisonous plants.
4. Shelter from hot sun and flies, and from wet and windy weather.
5. A daily check to make certain the pony has not been caught up in wire, or suffered any obvious cuts or injuries. This daily check is even more important if he is wearing a cover and/or a halter. At least once a week, even if he is not being ridden, he should be caught and examined thoroughly.
6. If he is shod, his feet will need attention every four to six weeks. If unshod, his feet must be examined regularly, and trimmed with a rasp if the horn is breaking away and becoming ragged, or the feet are growing too long (see shoeing, page 152).
7. Space in which to move about and stretch his legs, and to allow for more variety in grazing. If he has to live in a small paddock he must have regular exercise, and a change of paddock whenever possible.
8. Company — preferably of his own kind but, failing that, almost any animal will do as a companion.
9. Regular worming and attention to his teeth (see page 163).

What To Look For When Choosing A Paddock

1. Water. A paddock which is ideal in all other respects simply will not do if the water supply is inadequate. Water may be supplied by:

(a) A trough with a ballcock which allows it to fill up as the pony drinks. This is probably the best method of all, provided there are no sharp edges or projections such as taps, on which the pony could get caught up.

(b) A running stream or a dam — quite satisfactory so long as it doesn't become boggy in winter and dry up in summer. If the bottom is muddy or sandy, this could cause colic.

(c) A washing-machine bowl or other large receptacle which can be filled from a hosepipe. Also quite satisfactory, provided the receptacle has no sharp edges which would cause injury, and provided it is kept clean and filled up regularly.

Trying to keep a pony supplied from buckets of water which have to be carried to the paddock is really a discouraging proposition, especially in hot weather, when he may drink up to forty litres a day!

2. Sound and safe fences and gates. Paddocks with wire fences are quite all right so long as the wire is tight. Loose, loopy wire is extremely dangerous — it is probably the cause of more injuries to horses and ponies than any other single factor. Plain No 8 wire is much safer than either barbed or the 12-gauge high-tensile wire. Thick, solid

A contrast in paddocks:

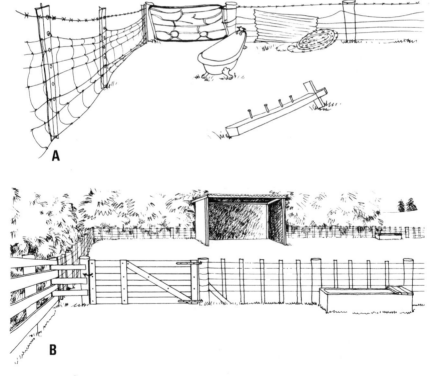

A It will not be 'bad luck' if your pony comes to grief here.
B Everything a pony could wish for — safe fences and gate, shelter and water.

hedges are good, providing shelter as well as security, but beware of the thorny varieties such as barberry or hawthorn. Gates must open easily and fully, and have secure fastenings. It may, of course, be possible to have fences and gates repaired or replaced if the paddock is otherwise suitable, but this can be a very costly process. Continual do-it-yourself patching-up is frustrating in the extreme.

3. Feed. Study the vegetation carefully — this is what your pony will have to live on. First check for any of the poisonous plants — such as ragwort — and for weeds such as thistles, barley grass, docks or penny-royal. Rushes and buttercups indicate that the paddock is likely to be wet in winter, even if it is dry at the moment. Look for a good mixture of grasses, and a reasonable amount of clover, but remember that over-rich grazing can cause laminitis, or founder, in ponies — one of the most painful diseases they can get (see page 164).

Generally a rolling or slightly hilly paddock will carry better feed than a flat, low-lying one. It is also better for the pony's feet, gives him more exercise and some shelter from the wind. Poor grazing can certainly be improved, but it is not easy to do this if you are only going to run ponies in the paddock. The necessary sprays and fertilisers will be expensive, and you will have to be prepared for a lot of hard work.

4. Space. With careful management it is just possible to keep a small pony on about a quarter of a hectare (about half an acre) but a bigger paddock would be much better. Ponies in their natural state are wide-ranging animals, and they really do like to have room to move about freely.

5. Shelter. May be supplied by large trees (check for low branches which could damage the pony's eyes), hedges, or undulating ground. If there is a shed, make sure that it is open to the front, built backing on to the prevailing wind, and high enough (minimum 2.5 metres). A windbreak in the form of a wooden wall about 2 metres high can be useful when no other shelter is available.

Elementary Care Of Pony Paddocks

However good your paddock is when you take it over, it will not stay that way without regular care on your part. The following are all very important:

Pick up any rubbish lying about, particularly glass, loose wire, or plastic bags. Fill in any holes that may appear, with stones and soil, well stamped in.

Check the water supply daily, especially in hot weather. Drinking troughs and bowls must be cleaned out regularly, or green slime will begin to appear on them. A handful of epsom salts helps to keep the water clear in troughs that cannot be emptied and cleaned out easily.

Check fences and gates frequently, and deal with anything that needs it as soon as possible — the longer you leave it, the bigger the eventual repair job! Never climb over fences or gates, or swing on gates.

It is difficult to keep paddocks in good heart if they are grazed only by ponies, because ponies are choosy feeders, eating only the grasses they like and leaving everything else until it becomes coarse and rank. If their droppings are left lying in heaps as they fall, they will sour the ground for some distance all round, and the paddock can quickly become 'horse-sick' and infested with red worm. If it is possible to graze other animals, particularly cattle, with the ponies, this will help a lot, as cattle will eat the rough grass the ponies leave, and will also break the worm cycle. Ponies and cattle will eat over and around one another's droppings, but not over their own.

In small paddocks — under half a hectare (about one acre) — picking up droppings is a necessary, if unpopular, chore. Try to do it every day — it is hard work if you leave it for a few days. (Don't forget the manure can be a valuable commodity that can help to pay the rent of your paddock.)

In larger paddocks, when you go out wearing your gumboots, either in frosty or in hot and sunny weather kick any heaps of droppings that you pass. Once they are spread out, the cold or heat will soon kill the worms. This would not happen if it was damp and humid, when you might only succeed in spreading the worms.

Topdressing. The amount of grass a paddock produces can be greatly increased by suitable manures. Lime is always good for sweetening horse paddocks, and tends to discourage worms by reducing the acidity of the soil. Apart from this, it would be best to ask a farmer neighbour or your local stock and station agents what manure is needed in your district, how much you should put on, and when. Grass is only of value when it is growing, so anything you can do to keep it coming away will be invaluable. Harrowing, and topping if the grass becomes long and stalky, can be most useful, but you would need advice and assistance with this, too.

Subdivision. Another thing to ask advice on. If it is possible to subdivide the paddock it can help to make the grass go further, as one part can be thoroughly cleaned up and rested while the pony is grazing the other part. Don't forget that water and shelter must be available in both sections.

Town sections (of about 1000 sq. m.) present many problems apart from their small size. Among these problems are:
1. Water — rarely laid on.

2. Feed. The land has probably been neglected for years, and will grow every kind of noxious weed much more willingly than it will grow grass.

3. Rubbish of all kinds thrown into the paddock. Well-meaning people may offer the pony lawn mowings, hedge-clippings and other things which could make him very ill or kill him.

4. Vandalism. People chasing, teasing or riding the pony. The gate may have to be padlocked at both ends to prevent his removal.

5. Where can you ride if the section is in a heavily built up area?

Care Of Pony With The Change Of Seasons

Spring. September-November. (Northern hemisphere equivalents are March–May.) Ponies tend to be at their lowest at the end of winter, especially if grass has been rather short. In many places they will still need hay, and possibly hard feed, during September (March), until the grass reaches its maximum growth in October (April). If your pony is rather light in condition, try to give him a holiday for a few weeks, to let him pick up on the spring grass. On the other hand, if he is the type who runs to fat, you may have to shut him up in a yard part of the time, to prevent him overeating and giving himself laminitis. If the pony is covered, take his cover off on warm days, so that he can roll and get rid of his winter coat. Scraping both the pony and the lining of the cover as often as possible with a rubber or plastic curry comb also helps with this.

Summer. December–February. (Northern hemisphere equivalents are June–August.) Some hard feed may be needed if the pony is working hard during the holidays. If the grass dries up and almost disappears in a dry spell, the pony will have to have hay to supply the necessary bulk. The daily water-supply check is particularly important in these conditions.

This is the time of year when you can really groom your pony thoroughly, and he should look very glossy in his summer coat. Try to remove bot eggs daily.

Unshod ponies' feet will need watching, especially if the ground is rough as well as hard. Be careful of doing too much jumping or fast work if the ground is hard — especially if your pony is under five years old.

Autumn. March–May. (Northern hemisphere equivalent September–October.) Have the pony dosed for bots and also for worms, about two weeks after the bot flies have disappeared. Get the vet to check his teeth, so that he will be able to get the best out of his winter feed. This is especially important with older ponies. Watch the pony's condition and the state of the pasture, and start to feed him the moment you notice any shortage of grass. There is often quite a flush of grass in the autumn once it rains, but in most places hay will be needed by late May (October) or early June, (November) at the latest. It is very difficult to replace condition lost in the autumn during the winter months.

Winter. June–August. (Northern hemisphere equivalent November–February.) Hay will be needed during this time in almost any temperate climate. Young or old ponies, or those in hard work, will almost certainly need hard feed as well.

Grooming should be confined to removing dried mud and sweat, as the pony needs the grease in his coat for warmth, particularly if he is not covered. If you ride after school and have difficulty in getting the pony dry before nightfall, he should be given a belly clip or a low trace clip (see page 149), but more than this is not recommended. On no account should small ponies be clipped 'right out'.

In cold districts you will have to break the ice on your pony's water trough night and morning. Ponies cannot break even thin ice for themselves. If the grass vanishes under snow, you will have to double the hay ration. Keep up the extra feed when the thaw comes because it will probably still be cold and wet, and what grass emerges will be soggy and of little food value.

SHUTTING UP FAT PONIES

It is dangerous to his health to allow a pony to become too fat — see page 136. Small ponies are especially prone to this problem, and nearly always need shutting up during the grass-growth period. However, it is important that the pony should receive sufficient bulk to keep his system working safely and also to prevent him from becoming sour.

Requirements:

1. A yard in which he can move freely and lie down.
2. Water always available. A pony must NEVER be kept short of water.
3. A small quantity (about 1.5 to 2 kilograms) of light meadow hay — for bulk and to relieve boredom.
4. A small feed of pony pellets and chaff *may* be needed, depending on work.
5. The pony must be allowed out for half to one hour night and morning, possibly longer if the paddock is suitable.

Tethering, page 143, offers an alternative for some ponies.

10
WATERING, FEEDING AND EXERCISE: C CERTIFICATE

WATERING

WATER is one of the most important things in a pony's life. No matter how well he is fed, he will not keep healthy, or even live for long without it. If water is always available, he can help himself whenever he is thirsty.

If you are out for a long day, take every opportunity to water your pony. If it is during a check at a hunt, for instance, and he is very hot, let him have only two or three swallows; but if he is cool and you will be going slowly for the next half hour or so, you may allow him to drink his fill.

Remember to water him during the day at shows and gymkhanas, though not just before an event.

On returning home after a long day, it is best to put the pony out in the paddock for about fifteen minutes before feeding him. This gives him time to settle down and have a roll and a drink. If he has a big drink after his feed, there is a danger that the food could be washed straight through his stomach into the intestine, and this could cause colic.

FEEDING

A pony's food has to do a number of things. The main ones are:

To keep him in good condition, round and well covered but not too fat, with a bright eye, a loose skin and a shiny coat.

To keep him warm, especially as he gets older.

To give him enough energy for the work he has to do.

To supply everything needed for bone growth and development in a young pony.

Ponies living in large paddocks with other stock are the most fortunate. For much of the year they will get all they need from the pasture and, when feeding-out is necessary, they will be fed along with the other animals. Extra feed will only be needed if the ponies are working very hard — hunting, eventing, or going to shows frequently. It is important to remember that a paddock which supplies all the pony's needs through the winter will supply far too much when the flush of spring growth comes. If he is allowed unrestricted grazing at this time he will soon get too fat, particularly on 'cow pastures', which are often too rich for ponies.

Supplementary feeding. This is of two kinds: bulk feeds (grass and hay); and concentrates or 'hard feed'.

Hay, of course, is dried grass or other fodder plants. Lucerne and hays with a very high proportion of clover are usually too rich for ponies, especially the smaller ones. Just as a pony will do very well on good average pasture, so meadow hay, containing a certain amount of clover and the grasses you look for in your paddock, is the obvious substitute when grass runs short. The following table shows what to look for and what to avoid when choosing hay.

	GOOD	BAD
Colour	Greenish to brownish.	Yellow or greyish. The latter indicates mildew.
Smell	Sweet, but not too strong — like silage, for instance.	Sour or musty.
Content	Good grasses, as in paddock. Clover up to about 30%. A fair proportion of seed-heads, not all stalks.	Ragwort — especially poisonous when dried in hay. Thistles, docks, pennyroyal, rushes, and buttercups. Weed seeds will pass straight through the pony's digestive system to come out in his droppings and germinate in the paddock.
Feel	Crisp and hard.	Soft and 'woolly'. Dusty hay is bad for a pony's digestion and for his wind.

Grass and hay supply the bulk that all horses and ponies *must have* to satisfy their appetites and to keep their digestions in good order. Without this bulk, even if they are 'hard fed' they will feel hungry, will lose condition and suffer from constipation. Very small ponies and those in light work may do quite well on grass and hay only.

Hard feed consists mainly of various types of grain. These are the energy and body-building foods which may be needed by:

Young ponies, for growth and bone development.

Older ponies — say from twelve years onwards — for warmth as well as for energy.

Ponies in hard work, who use up more energy than is generally supplied by grass and hay.

Ponies who are sick or out of condition, who will require special feeding.

Here are some of the main items of hard feed:

1. Horse and pony pellets, nuts or cubes. These are specially formulated to supply a balanced diet for horses and ponies, and are the best basic hard feed for ponies — easy to store and feed. They contain a variety of the grains listed below, usually not oats, plus linseed, molasses, vitamins and minerals. It is always advisable to mix them with a double handful of chaff, as there can be a danger of the pellets compacting and forming a solid mass in the pony's stomach, especially if he eats large quantities of wet grass or has a big drink of water immediately after a feed of pellets. Check that you get the correct grade, as there are different recipes for racehorses, brood mares and ponies.

2. Horse and pony ration consists of much the same formula as pellets, but is in the form of meal. Should also be mixed with chaff.

3. Dairy ration is sometimes fed to ponies and some of them do quite well on it. However, it is primarily intended for milking cows, and is really more suitable for them than for horses and ponies.

4. Chaff is of two kinds — oaten chaff and hay (usually lucerne) chaff. Oaten chaff is chopped oat straw, containing an uncertain quantity of oats. It is often an expensive feed, and may make your pony too lively. Hay or lucerne chaff is excellent. It discourages the pony from bolting his feed and provides bulk and fibre, which are essential for good digestion. As mentioned above, chaff also helps to prevent pellets or dairy ration from forming a solid mass in the stomach.

5. Bran is the husk of the wheat grain. It is a bulk food, slightly fattening, and useful as a laxative when well damped. It is easily digested, and is mainly used in the feeding of older or thin ponies. A bran mash is excellent for a sick pony, or for any pony after a hard day's work.

To make a bran mash. Put ½ to 1 kilo of bran into a large bucket, add a tablespoonful of common salt, and pour over about 1 litre of boiling water. Stir thoroughly with a stick — the mixture should be just crumbly, not soggy. Cover with a thick sack and leave for half an hour to steam. Then mix again by hand, making sure it is only just warm when you give it to the pony.

6. Wheat — apart from bran — is not a suitable pony food. It is indigestible, and its use can cause serious colic.

7. Barley. An energy food, not as exciting as oats (see below) and a most useful fattening food. Barley is too hard for ponies to chew, so it must be either boiled or crushed. Fed boiled, it is a winter feed, especially for older ponies. Crushed barley can be fed at any time, but it is not as easily digested as boiled barley.

To boil barley. Soak overnight, then boil slowly until just soft. Add salt for flavour. Mix with bran, if available, and steam, as for a bran mash. Otherwise mix the barley with two or three good double handfuls of chaff. Make sure you don't feed it too hot.

8. Oats are the best energy food of all, but they are not suitable for small ponies, who nearly always become excitable and difficult to ride when fed oats. They may be useful for lazy or hard-working ponies, but should not be fed unless advised by an experienced person. Oats are best fed lightly bruised, so that the husk is just cracked. If fed whole, they tend to go right through the pony in their original state; if crushed too much, a large part of the flour and the goodness is lost. Once crushed, they must be fed within a month.

9. Maize is a highly concentrated food, not really suitable for ponies, though small quantities, as contained in pellets, will do no harm. Maize must never be fed whole.

10. Extras. These are not basic foods, but they are juicy or flavoursome additions to the diet which most ponies enjoy. They are particularly useful for sick ponies, or for shy feeders. They include:

Linseed. Fattening and very good for putting a shine on the coat. Whole linseed *must* be boiled, otherwise it is poisonous. Crushed linseed need not be boiled, but does not keep well. If pellets are fed, extra linseed is rarely necessary.

Molasses. Fattening, and almost as sweet as sugar. Liquid molasses is messy to handle — the powdered form is much easier and just as good for the pony.

Carrots provide some energy — most useful in winter, when there is less nourishment in the grass. Always feed sliced lengthways, not in chunks, which could choke a pony.

Apples should not be fed in large quantities, but are useful as a titbit, or when catching.

Bread is most indigestible in large quantities, and should not be fed as a staple food. The odd slice as a titbit is quite in order.

Salt is a necessity of life for all animals. Best supplied by a lump of rock salt or iodised salt lick in the paddock, so that the pony can help himself when he feels the need. If not available in this form, salt *must* be added to the feed of ponies in hard work, to replace the salt lost in sweat.

Note: All these 'extras' should be used in moderation, and not all at once in the same feed, which would produce a very sickly mixture!

WHEN AND HOW TO FEED

Few ponies will need to be fed more than once a day, unless they are sick, are working very hard, or in extreme weather conditions.

The best time to feed is late afternoon or early evening, after the pony has finished work for the day. This gives him plenty of time to eat and digest his food, and a full stomach will help to keep him warm through the night in cold weather. If two feeds are given, the main part of the ration should still be given at night, with a smaller feed as early as possible in the morning.

Hay

Hay may be fed in three ways: from the ground, in a haynet, or from a hayrack or feeder.

1. From the ground. This is really the most practical, though there may be some wastage from trampling. If much hay is being wasted in this way, obviously the amount given should be cut down. The following rules should be observed:

(a) Never put hay close to the gate, to fence lines, to any permanent jumps in the paddock, or in a corner.

(b) If the weather is bad, feed in the driest and most sheltered spot — usually where the pony himself chooses to stand.

(c) In dry weather, put the hay on any bare patches in the paddock, where the seeds will germinate and improve the pasture.

(d) Always put out more piles of hay than there are ponies, and put the piles at least three lengths apart — out of kicking distance. This will ensure that everyone gets his share, safely.

(e) Shake out the hay and damp it, if it is at all dusty.

2. Haynets are excellent for feeding a pony in a yard or stable, or when travelling, but are not so suitable for use in the paddock.

3. Hayracks can be convenient, but they often lead to fighting and kicking, especially where large numbers of ponies are involved. The ground around them soon becomes cut up, unless the racks can be moved easily and frequently.

Hard Feed

1. Use a strong, heavy container with no sharp edges, such as a washing-machine bowl or a solid wooden or plastic box. One for each pony.

2. See rules (a) and (b) above, for feeding hay from the ground. They apply to hard feed, too.

3. Put all ingredients into a bucket, damp slightly, mix well and tip into feed container. Do not feed from the bucket.

4. Always keep containers clean, especially after bran mashes or boiled feed.

5. Remove any leftover food — never mix it with fresh.

Note: It is most important that all ponies in a paddock are fed at the same time. If some ponies are getting hard feed, they must be taken out and fed somewhere else. Trying to fend off angry ponies who are *not* supposed to be receiving hard feed creates an extremely dangerous situation for all concerned.

1 No way out!

2A: Winner takes all!

2B: Peace and safety.

I

2a

2b

HOW MUCH TO FEED

Supplementary Feed

It should be clear by now that the amount and type of supplementary feed a pony needs depend on a number of factors.

The most important of these are:

1. The pony himself — his size, age, type, temperament, and his condition and state of health.
2. The quality and quantity of grass available in his paddock.
3. The work required of him.
4. Your own experience and ability as a rider.

We shall now consider these factors individually.

1. (a) Size. Obviously a 147.5 cm pony will need more feed than a 117.5 cm and a 167.5 cm horse will need a great deal more still, but it does depend on other things as well:

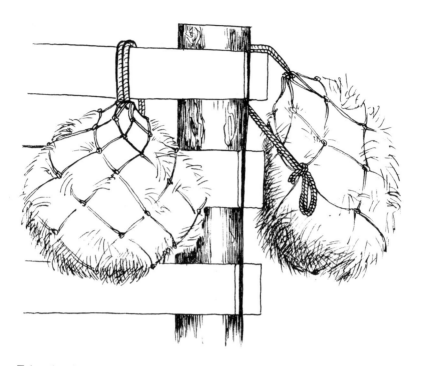

Tying the drawstring through a lower mesh of the net helps to adjust height, so that, when it is empty, there is no risk of the pony getting his feet entangled. Use a quick-release knot and tie to something solid. Turn the net so that the knot is underneath.

(b) Age. Young and old, as we have seen, need more than those in the prime of life. Young ponies, especially if they are working, need food for growth and development, as well as maintenance of condition. Suitable foods are the brood-mare grade of pellets, skim-milk powder and carrots. Not too much bran (because of its high phosphorous content). Older ponies (say 12-plus need extra food for warmth. Pellets, bran, and boiled barley or oats in cold weather are particularly good for them. Lucerne chaff is excellent for both young and old.

(c) Type and temperament. There is less variation in small ponies, but the bigger ponies and horses range from the solid, cobby type to the highly-strung thoroughbred or Arab. The former are often the ones who 'get fat on the smell of an oily rag' — it is especially important to limit their access to rich spring grass. Avoid fattening foods such as bran, molasses, and boiled barley, but when working harder, they may benefit from some oats. The excitable thoroughbred types take much more out of themselves in their work, and sometimes, even in the paddock, 'walking the fence' and never really settling down,

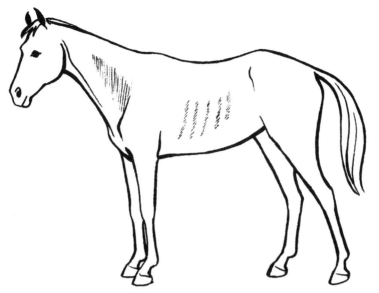

Young and poor. Needs 'maintenance-plus' for growth and development, and to build him up into good condition.

No worries! Maintenance ration.

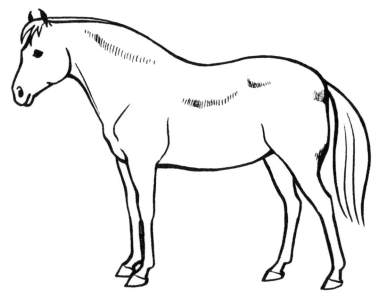

Too fat. Note how the fat builds up on the neck and over the back. Must have 'maintenance-minus' until his figure improves.

either to graze or to rest. Fattening foods are fine for them — oats will only make them even more jumpy. To replace all the nervous energy they use up, they will need more food for their size than the 'slow-solid' ones.

(d) Condition and state of health. If the pony is well in himself and just right in condition, he needs a 'maintenance ration' to keep him as he is. If he is too thin, you must first try to find out why (page 162) but, whatever the reason, he will need 'maintenance-plus', so that the surplus will gradually build him up into good condition. If too fat, he must have 'maintenance-minus' (but not to the point of starvation), so that his system will be forced to burn up that dangerous excessive fat. The young pony needs 'maintenance-plus-growth' rations, the older one 'maintenance-plus-warmth'. In fact, any pony will need extra feed in extremely cold conditions. If a pony is obliged to supply growth, warmth or the energy needed for hard work from a maintenance ration, he will lose condition.

2. The Paddock
This is really the crux of the matter when it comes to keeping horses and ponies at grass. Almost any paddock will supply a maintenance ration for a pony in the flush of spring grass — most paddocks much

more, so that the pony needs to be shut up for part of the time. Apart from this, the same paddock can vary tremendously from year to year, according to the stock it is carrying, whether or not it has been topdressed and, above all, the weather. If it is wet, the grass may continue to grow right through the summer and well into the autumn, but in winter the ground will 'pug up' and much of the grass will be trampled into mud. If it is too dry, there will be little or no growth in summer or autumn, but although the grass appears sparse, ponies may still do well on it. Early autumn frosts probably knock grass back more quickly than anything, and can force one to start feeding hay several weeks earlier than would be necessary in a milder year. Constant observation is your only guide — observation of the state of the grass, the condition of the pony, his behaviour, and his state of fitness for the work he has to do.

Always try to think ahead. Start feeding hay before the paddock is completely bare; if you know your pony is going to have a busy time during the holidays, start feeding him at least two weeks beforehand.

3. The Work Required Of The Pony
Most ponies and horses will probably be able to do light work — about an hour a day at steady paces — on a maintenance ration, but when harder and faster work is required, the energy used will burn up more food. Unless a working pony is given 'maintenance-plus-energy' rations, he will lose condition, and will certainly not become fit and muscular with the increased work.

Energy food, as we have seen, is hard feed, which is essential for ponies that are: hunting; eventing; going regularly to shows or gymkhanas; or for long rides, especially in hilly country, or to Pony Club camp or on courses. Grass will supply a maintenance ration, sometimes all the year round for small ponies, but it does not supply enough energy for the above activities. It is quite unfair to your pony to expect him to take part in them without sufficient feed of the right kind. On his day off, or whenever the work is cut down for any reason, reduce the hard feed and substitute more bulk, if necessary.

4. Your Own Experience And Ability As A Rider
The food he eats can change a pony's character, as well as his physique, completely. Even the quietest pony can become quite lively and excitable when the fresh grass comes through in the spring, or if he is given too much hard feed, particularly oats, at any time. When you are a beginner, your pony will only be getting light, steady work, so he will only need a maintenance ration.

But as your riding improves and you want to do more active and adventurous things with him, he will have to be fed accordingly.

More work, and the feed that goes with it, will gradually make the pony fitter, in the sense that an athlete is 'fit'. A fit pony is usually harder to ride than the same pony when he is well but not fit. When fit, he may buck, kick or shy when he is fresh, and will probably take a stronger hold when galloping and jumping.

As you get fitter yourself, as your seat strengthens and your confidence grows, you may find that you can enter into the fun with him and thoroughly enjoy all this. But if you feel it is too much to cope with, you must adjust both feed and work until he returns to a more manageable state.

You will realise from the foregoing how extremely difficult it is to lay down exact rations for any pony or horse without knowing about all these factors which affect his requirements. The charts on page 140 are intended only as a very rough guide and a starting point. We suggest that you make a similar table for your own pony, then pick out the nearest one from this selection and work out his ration, making due allowance for variations in size of paddock, age of pony, amount of work, etc.

RULES FOR GOOD FEEDING

Finally, bear in mind these rules for good feeding:

1. Feed plenty of bulk. As already explained, your pony's digestion cannot function properly without it. He may need hard feed, he must have bulk.

2. Feed regularly, at the same time *every* day. Ponies seem to have an 'internal clock', and will soon begin to get restless if their feed is not forthcoming at the time they expect it. If several ponies are kept waiting together, this is when kicking matches are liable to start.

3. Don't work your pony immediately after a feed, or on bringing him in from grass. It will give him indigestion, and will make him blow a lot. This is because his stomach lies close to his lungs and, when full, it will prevent him from expanding his lungs properly. This can lead to an incurable condition of the lungs known as 'broken wind'. It takes a pony about twenty minutes to eat a hard feed, and at least an hour to digest it. He should be given longer than this if he is going to do any fast work.

4. Don't make sudden changes in feeding. Introduce any new type of feed — especially oats — very gradually, beginning with not more than half a kilo a day, and only increasing it a little at a time.

5. Feed according to the work the pony is doing and his condition from day to day. If his work is cut down, especially if this is due to sickness or injury, cut down the hard feed and replace it with bulk food.

6. Weigh the feed, so that you can adjust quantities easily and

accurately according to the pony's condition and behaviour.

7. Feed the best quality forage you can get — if in doubt, ask advice before buying. Remember that any grain, once crushed, 'goes off' quickly.

8. Always water before feeding. See page 128.

EXERCISE

Ponies, like people, need exercise if they are to remain healthy. When you are a beginner, the pony will get his exercise from the things you do in the course of learning to ride. One of the most important things, from both your own point of view and the pony's, is that this riding should be regular. It is no use to either of you to leave the pony out in the paddock for weeks and then 'ride the tail off him' all day when the holidays come. He would get tired, sore, and probably rather cross.

Of course, it may be that you get back from school too late to ride during the week in the winter, and so for some months of the year you can only ride at weekends. But just remember that a pony is neither a machine, nor a toy to be played with all day when you have time. He will not be very fit if he is only ridden at weekends, especially if he lives in a small paddock where he hasn't much room to exercise himself. So ride him either in the morning or the afternoon, then put him back in the paddock to graze and rest.

There may be occasional all-day activities, such as a rally, gymkhana or hunt, but if you know something of this kind is coming up, you should make a big effort to ride more regularly for a week or two beforehand. Generally, riding morning or afternoon but not all day is a good rule. A pony should have one 'day off' a week.

A wide variety of work and play is essential to keep up the interest of pony and rider. The riding chapters of this book should give you plenty of ideas for this. Don't forget that constant galloping about and jumping is hard work for the pony, however much you may enjoy it — he needs quiet exercise at a walk and steady trot as well.

As the demands you make on your pony in his work increase and you want to go to shows, horse trials or hunts, exercise as well as training becomes still more important — just as it does for you if you are a member of a hockey or football team. You will find suggestions for fitness and training for different events in the 'Competitions' chapter. Under 'Horse Trials' we have explained the difference between 'work' and 'exercise'.

EXAMPLES OF SUPPLEMENTARY FEED TABLES

Age, size, type of pony/horse.	Paddock	Work	Ability of rider	Season		SUGGESTED SUPPLEMENTARY FEED
1. (a) 4 years, 147.5cm, quiet temperament. Broken, starting training.	2 hectares average grazing	Ridden most days. Schooling, early jumping, PC.	Experienced	Spring summer	—	1kg pellets, chaff, Bone-gro or vitamin/mineral supplement. Hay if needed. Increase pellets to 2kg if working harder or grass short.
				Autumn winter	—	Hay as needed, 1-2kg pellets, extras, vit/min supplement. Hay as needed (4-5kg). ½-1kg boiled barley with bran and chaff, once or twice weekly. Other days, 2kg pellets, chaff, extras.
(b) Same, now 6-8 years	Same	Ridden most days	Beginner	Spring summer	—	None, except possibly if grass dries up in summer.
				Autumn winter	—	Hay as needed. Midwinter — 1kg pellets, chaff, extras ½-1kg crushed or boiled barley, twice weekly.
(c) Same, now 9-12 years	Same	PC camp and trek. Course, novice PC Horse Trials. Hunts. Ridden most days.	Same. Now good C+	Summer holidays, dry spell	—	Hay as needed, 1-2kg oats, 1kg pellets, chaff, extras divided into two feeds.
				Autumn winter	—	Feed as above, adjusted according to condition and behaviour. Boiled barley twice weekly. Bran mash after hunts, etc.
(d) Same, now 13+	Same	Ridden most days. PC camp, etc.	Beginner Younger sister	Summer holidays	—	Hay if needed, 2kg pellets, chaff, extras.
				Winter		Hay as needed, boiled barley with ½-1kg bran, chaff 4-5 times weekly. Pellets, chaff, extras other days.

The object of this table is to show how the requirements of a good-average pony, living throughout mainly in the same paddock, can vary as he is ridden by different members of the family during his working life.

Age, size, type of pony/horse.	Paddock	Work	Ability of rider	Season		SUGGESTED SUPPLEMENTARY FEED
2. 6-12 years, 125cm approx. Runs to fat.	¾ hectare rough pasture	Ridden weekends and sometimes in week.	Beginner	Spring summer	—	None — possibly a little hay if grass very short.
				Autumn winter	—	Possibly hay if grass very short. Hay — 3-4kg. If very cold, ½kg pellets, chaff, extras.
3. 10 years, 157.5-167.5cm. ex-racehorse or trotter. Excitable	1 hectare bare	Ridden most days, 1 hour approx.	Beginner 14+	Spring summer Autumn	—	Hay if needed. 2kg pellets, ½-1kg crushed barley extras. Hay. Feed as above, plus ½-1kg bran, 3-4 times weekly.
				Winter		Hay, 5-7kg, 3kg pellets, chaff, extras. Boiled barley and bran 4 times weekly. Two feeds daily.

Combination No. 3 is not recommended — not a suitable type of horse for a beginner. He will have been hard fed from weaning, and cannot possibly live in a small paddock of this kind without hard feed — NOT oats. He will be an expensive animal to keep, and you must realise this before you buy him.

11
HANDLING, GROOMING, SHOEING: C CERTIFICATE

HANDLING

Safety Factors

REMEMBER that even a small pony is a large and heavy animal. Whether he is shod or not, he still has very sharp feet. He is a creature of flight, and the quietest pony can move like greased lightning if suddenly startled. If you always bear the following safety factors in mind, you should avoid unnecessary accidents:

Never stand directly in front of any pony, or directly behind one that you don't know well — for instance, when brushing the tail.

When approaching a pony, do so from the front, towards his shoulder. Speak before touching him, so that he knows you are there.

Always were solid boots or shoes around ponies. Never sit, kneel or crawl underneath the pony. When brushing the legs, bend or squat down, so that you can move quickly if need be.

When holding or leading a pony, never twist the rope round your hand. Don't leave loose ends of rope or reins trailing on the ground, where you or the pony could get tangled up in them. Never allow a led pony to go in front of you, out to the end of the rope.

When tying up, keep your fingers out of any loops while tying the knot. Preferably tie to a piece of string. Never tie to anything movable, such as a branch of a tree, a jump stand, or an unattached float.

LEADING IN HAND

See page 38, in 'Care of the Pony, D Certificate', and safety factor number four above. To lead at the trot: first get the pony walking up well, with his shoulder level with yours. Say 'Trot on' rather sharply as you begin to run. If he hangs back, put the rope into the hand nearest to the pony, and have your riding whip or a long switch in the other hand. Reach round behind yourself and tap the pony on the ribs. Be ready to steady him if he shoots forward, and praise him when he trots beside you.

If he tries to swing away, put him up against a fence-line, so that he is between you and the fence. Alternatively, you could get somebody to encourage him, as quietly as possible, from behind.

Apart from its uses for gymkhana events, it is important to teach your pony to lead freely in hand, so that you can 'run him up in hand' if you suspect that he may be lame.

LOADING A QUIET PONY

Before loading, the float, the towing vehicle and the coupling must be checked every time by the driver or other experienced person — see *Pony Club Manual No 2* .

The pony should have a halter on, with a good length of rope. He should never be saddled and bridled when travelling. Covers may or may not be needed, depending on the weather, whether the float is open or closed, and whether the pony is usually covered. Bandages or travelling boots will probably not be necessary for short trips in a single float, or in a double one with a solid partition down to floor level. A tail bandage may well be needed. All these matters are explained in the *Pony Club Manual No. 2* — if in doubt, ask at Pony Club.

Pony correctly tied up in float. Note length of rope, quick-release knot and binder twine.

142

Make sure that the float is on flat ground, so that the ramp will be steady. Have the access door in the front open, so that the pony can see right through, and you can get out that way. Open the centre partition as wide as possible for loading — if your pony is travelling alone, or is the first one to go on. If you are travelling only one pony in a double float, it is best to put him on the right-hand side. Have a titbit ready for him.

When you lead the pony on, have him straight on to the ramp, and walk on steadily and confidently yourself, without hesitating or looking back at him. As you enter the float, go in front of the pony and duck under the front rail. Give him his titbit and hold him until the back strap has been fastened and the ramp put up — on no account tie him up until this has been done. Use a quick-release knot; the rope should be long enough to let him reach his hay-net, if he has one, but not long enough to let him turn his head right round, or nip his neighbour in a double float.

UNLOADING

Get in and untie the pony, preferably before the ramp is lowered. He *must* be untied before the back strap is undone. Back him off slowly, taking care to keep him straight, so that he doesn't bump his hip on either side. Have somebody standing at the side to see that he continues straight as he comes down the ramp — if he stepped off before reaching the bottom he could injure himself.

Note: The importance of having a strong strap, chain or bar behind the pony cannot be over-stressed. This prevents him from backing off before the ramp is fully up or down. He must *never* be tied up in the float when this strap is undone.

TETHERING

No pony should ever be kept permanently tethered, but tethering for limited periods only can be useful. If feed is short in your paddock, it enables you to make use of unfenced, grassy areas, or it can be used as a part-time restriction for the very fat pony, if no yard is available. It must only be considered for quiet ponies, and even they need constant supervision. Water must always be available.

Incorrect tethering can be extremely dangerous, so seek expert advice on whether your pony and the area where you propose to tether him are suitable, and about the equipment needed.

CARE OF THE PONY BEFORE AND AFTER RIDING

Before

Brush your pony over before you ride him, as you have always done. You should be able to do it more thoroughly by now, and to pick out his feet for yourself (see pages 145-9 for grooming).

While grooming, check the pony over carefully. If you find any of the following, you should not ride him until you have asked advice from an experienced person:

A runny nose or a cough.

Any eye injury, especially if the eye is swollen or closed up.

Any but a very slight cut or kick.

A twisted (sprung) shoe, or badly raised clenches, especially on the inside. If he has cast a shoe, provided the foot hasn't broken away, he may be ridden on grass, but should not be taken on the road (see pages 150–4 for shoeing).

Any swelling and/or heat or pain up his tendons (see page 160).

Any lameness.

A sore mouth or back, or a bad girth gall. If he has a raw gall he can only be ridden bareback until it has healed.

Any dull or out-of-sorts appearance.

Riding a pony when he shows any of the above symptoms may not only cause him discomfort; it may make the condition much worse and cause him to be off work for a long time.

After A Ride

Always try to bring the pony in cool. If he is damp under the saddle, slacken the girth and lift the saddle off his back for a moment, but leave it on while you attend to the rest of him. Remove the bridle and tie the pony up. Pick out feet again, and check shoes. Brush over, paying particular attention to behind the ears, the nose, where the noseband has been, between the forelegs, under the stomach and between the hindlegs. Then remove the saddle; if the saddle patch is still damp, rub vigorously with a towel, finishing with a brush, the way of the hair. Brush the girth area thoroughly. Put on cover, if worn, and turn out.

After A Long Day

Be especially careful to bring the pony in cool. Treat as above, checking for injuries as you brush him over. Turn out, allowing about fifteen minutes for a drink and a roll before feeding. Next day, catch pony, check again for injuries and for soundness by running him up in hand (see page 160). Groom at least thoroughly enough to remove all dried mud and sweat, then put him back in the paddock and give him the day off.

Wet Days

If it is wet and you have nowhere to put the pony under cover, unsaddle and turn him out immediately. Even if it has stopped raining he will only get chilled standing about while you try to dry him. If he is covered, it is still best to put his cover on and turn him out at once; he will move around and keep warm, and will gradually dry off under the cover. If you have any hay or straw available, it helps to put a thick layer, well shaken out, on his back, under the. cover. This allows air to circulate and speeds up the drying process.

GROOMING

Ponies in regular work require grooming for the following reasons:
1. To keep the skin and coat healthy. Dried mud and sweat (a) cause girth galls and saddle sores, and (b) clog the pores of the skin and prevent it from sweating freely.
2. To provide massage, which stimulates circulation and muscle tone.
3. To improve appearance. A well-groomed pony is one of the best advertisements a caring rider can have, and an object of legitimate pride.

Grooming Method

1. Collect grooming kit, including a bucket of water. Tie pony up.
2. Pick out the feet. See illustrations and captions.
3. Brush the pony over with the dandy brush. Hold the brush correctly and make sure all mud and sweat are removed. Brush the heels carefully as mud left there could cause inflamation.
4. Mane and tail. Use a body brush or a *soft* dandy, never a curry comb.

Mane. Turn the mane over to the far side and brush the roots thoroughly. Turn it back to its correct side (whichever side it lies best, usually the right) and starting at the withers, separate a small piece; brush from the roots down, then let another piece go and repeat until finished. Any tangles should be worked out with the fingers. Brush out the forelock in the same way. Finally, brush the whole mane from root to tip until it lies tidily — it may help to 'lay' it with a damp brush.

Tail. Start by brushing the top of the tail thoroughly. Then separate the long hair piece by piece and brush downwards with long strokes. Be gentle with a soft tail — roughness or hard brushes will break the hair and ruin the tail. If it is tangled or very dirty, it is best to wash it to start with. Use warm water in your plastic bucket for this, wash with Sunlight soap and be sure to rinse it out thoroughly. If you have not seen this done, or your pony is not used to it, get help the first time.

(Continued page 147)

145

Grooming kit, as listed in text.

Grooming Kit

1. The hoof pick, for cleaning out the feet.
2. The dandy brush, for removing dried mud and sweat.
3. The body brush, for removing dust, scurf and grease from the coat, and for brushing the head, mane and tail.
4. The curry comb, primarily intended for cleaning the body brush. A rubber or plastic curry comb is preferable, as it can be used gently on the pony to remove caked mud and sweat, and to help to get his winter coat out in spring. A metal curry comb must *never* be used on the pony, and no curry comb should be used on head, mane or tail.
5. The water brush for washing the feet, and for 'laying' the mane and tail. A scrubbing brush, or even an old dandy, will do for this.
6. Two sponges, for cleaning the eyes, muzzle and dock.
7. Several towels, for drying off a damp pony, and putting on the final polish after grooming.
8. A small plastic bucket.
9. Hoof oil and brush — for special occasions, or for brittle feet.
10. Bot knife — for removing bot eggs.
11. Mane comb.
12. Small brush — useful at D level.

5. Sponge the eyes, nose, lips and dock. Use a damp sponge or a cloth kept for the purpose. It is preferable to keep a separate one for the dock.

Eyes. Sponge towards the tear duct, from the back towards the front, so that any dust or dirt will be wiped out of, not into, the eye.

Nose and lips must be cleaned thoroughly, but gently.

Dock. Stand to one side, lean over and lift the tail, and sponge the whole of the dock area, including the underside of the tail. These parts can become very dirty, and can attract flies in the summer, if neglected.

6. Hoof oil. Ponies with brittle feet should have their feet oiled daily. The feet are more likely to become brittle in the summer, especially if you ride much on the beach, or at any time if the wall of the foot has been rasped excessively. If the feet are muddy, it will be necessary to wash them first. Use your water brush for this; hold the foot up, pressing your thumb well into the hollow of the heel to keep the water out as much as possible. Let the foot dry before oiling.

A mixture of two parts of neatsfoot oil to one part of Stockholm tar is excellent. The oil should go up to the coronet, but not over it.

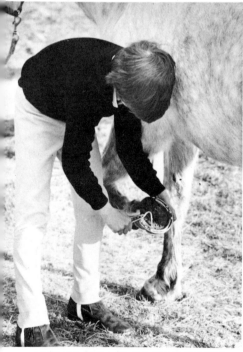

Hold the foot with the hand nearest to the pony. Use the hoof-pick from heel to toe to avoid damage to the frog.

Do not pull the hind leg back or out to the side.

Always pick up the foot and oil across the heels.

The pony should now be presentable for your daily ride, but if it is a special occasion, such as a rally or gymkhana, you could smarten his appearance still further by using the following:

7. The body brush. Unless you are getting the pony fit for competitions or for hunting, or are showing him, this is not essential for everyday use. Its purpose is to remove the grease from the coat. This grease helps to keep the pony warm and dry, so the body brush should not be used much in winter, unless you add an extra cover to compensate. In any case, it would not get through a thick winter coat.

It is a very different matter in summer, when the shorter bristles of the body brush will get right through and remove the layer of grease that lies close to the skin; it will really bring up the shine and tone up the pony's muscles (and yours too!).

To achieve this, the body brush must be used with long strokes, with plenty of weight behind it. After every three or four strokes, clean the brush by rubbing it across the curry comb. It is very satisfying to see how much grease you have collected when you knock out the curry comb at the end.

8. A slightly damp cloth or towel for a final polish, and to remove any scurf or dust remaining on the surface.

9. Feet should always be oiled when you want your pony to look smart. For very special occasions black boot-polish looks well on black feet, and won't attract dust. White feet should not be blacked — use plain neatsfoot oil, and rub up if necessary.

Plaiting

A well-plaited mane and tail certainly improve a pony's appearance, but plaiting takes a lot of practice. Until you can do it neatly, it would be better to turn your pony out with a clean, well-brushed mane and tail.

Remember that you must have done the plaiting yourself if your pony is plaited for a turnout class or for your C Certificate test. Judges and examiners are not interested in what your mother or anyone else can do!

For method of plaiting, see the *Pony Club Manual No. 2*, or ask to be shown how to do it at Pony Club.

Care Of Grooming Kit

Keep all your kit tidily together in the plastic bucket — never leave brushes lying around where the pony might step on them. Wash the brushes once a week — towels whenever they need it.

To wash brushes: use a weak solution of detergent and warm water. 'Dap' the bristles up and down in the solution, without getting the backs wet. Rinse in clear water in the same way, then stand the brushes bristles down to dry.

WASHING

Washing is not recommended as a regular way of keeping the pony clean. If done in cold conditions, especially after trials or hunting in winter, there is a great danger of chills, and constant washing will remove too much of the natural oil from the pony's coat.

However, in the late spring when ponies often seem to be especially dirty, a good wash with Triocel or a similar shampoo will enhance appearance and make the daily grooming easier. Be sure to choose a warm day, and do dry the pony thoroughly and keep him warm afterwards.

Sponging down sweaty areas, or even hosing a pony all over in really hot weather, is quite permissible, but care is needed, and there are several don'ts:

1. Don't wash or hose on a cold day, or in a chilly breeze.
2. Don't hose or wash late in the day.
3. Don't leave a wet pony tied up in a draught, especially under trees. Steady exercise will warm and dry him quickly.
4. Don't make a habit of washing white socks, and when you do wash them, use cold water. (Hot water will remove the protective grease and may cause cracked heels or mud fever.)
5. Don't use washing or hosing as a daily method of cleaning.

CLIPPING AND TRIMMING

These are fully covered in the *Manual No. 2*. They are subjects with which you will need help at this stage. Recommended clips are shown here. Never have your pony clipped 'right out' — (all over) unless he is stabled.

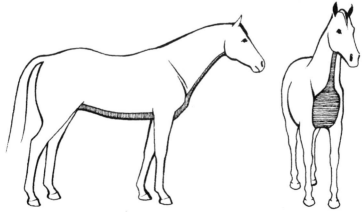

Recommended clips: Belly clip. Ideal for the horse or pony doing light work. The shaded areas are clipped.

Trace clip. Suitable for those doing more energetic work, such as hunting or one day events.

The Foot and Shoeing

The pony's foot consists of a hard, horny shell — the wall, the sole and the frog — surrounding and protecting the sensitive inner structures — bones, joints and blood vessels. When the foot has just been trimmed you can clearly see the 'white line' round the edge of the sole. This marks the division between the insensitive and sensitive parts of the foot. Any nails inside this line will cause pain and lameness.

The wall of the foot is growing down from the coronet all the time — it grows as our fingernails and toenails do. In the natural state a pony covers fairly large distances daily, mostly at slow paces and on firm, rather than hard, ground. This wears his feet down just about as fast as they grow, and all is well. Foot trouble is rare among the wild native ponies of the British Isles, for instance.

Most small ponies have strong, hard feet, and can certainly do light work without shoes, provided you keep off metal roads and other rough surfaces. Once they have been shod, it is usually necessary to continue shoeing, as the feet become softer.

If the unshod pony is not in regular work, particularly if he lives in a paddock where the ground is damp and the feed plentiful, his feet will grow quicker than they wear away. The toes get longer, finally turning upwards. This throws great strain on the back tendons, by putting too much weight on to the heels. The same thing happens to the shod pony if the shoes are left on too long.

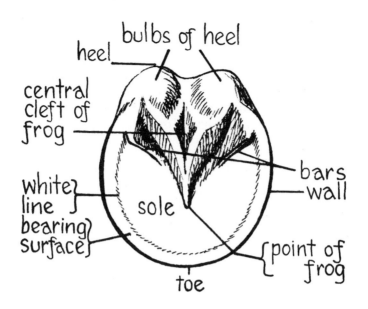

Parts of the foot.

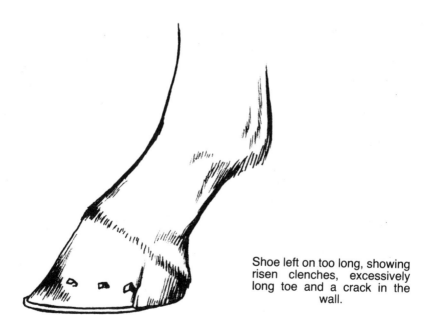

Shoe left on too long, showing risen clenches, excessively long toe and a crack in the wall.

Shoeing is necessary if the pony is ridden regularly on the road, or is required to do much jumping or faster work on hard ground, otherwise the feet will wear down faster than they grow, and bits of the wall may break off, leaving jagged edges. Before long the sensitive inner parts of the foot will be exposed, and he will become literally 'footsore'. Generally horses and bigger ponies have softer feet than the little ones, and few of them can do any but light work on soft ground without being shod.

HOW TO TELL WHEN YOUR PONY NEEDS SHOEING

1. If a shoe is twisted or half pulled off (called 'sprung'), particularly if nails are sticking up, or the shoe is sticking out on the inside. This could injure the pony severely, and you must keep him as still as possible until you can get somebody to take the shoe off.

2. If a shoe is loose, or if it is lost altogether — called 'cast'.

3. If a shoe is broken or worn very thin — this usually happens first at the toe.

4. If any clenches have risen. The clenches are the ends of the nails, where they are turned over on the wall of the foot. A risen clench is one that is sticking out, instead of lying flush with the foot. This is more serious on the inside, as the sharp edge can cut the opposite fetlock joint (see diagram Page 151).

5. If the foot has overgrown the shoe at any point, or the toes are growing too long.

6. If the shoes have slipped in at the heels and are pressing on the 'corn place', as shown in the picture. A corn in a pony is a painful bruise which occurs at this spot, and is usually caused by leaving the shoes on too long. If the shoes are worn, a new set will be needed but in many cases a 'remove' will suffice. This means that the shoes are taken off, the feet trimmed and the same shoes put on again.

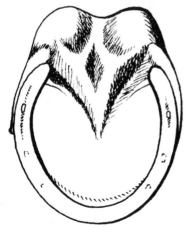

This shoe has also been left on too long, and has slipped into the 'corn place'.

152

TYPES OF SHOES

The picture shows the two main types of shoes — concaves and road shoes.

A concave shoe is made of bevelled steel, so that it is wider on the 'bearing surface' against the pony's foot, than on the ground surface. The shoes shown are also 'fullered' — there is a groove running round the ground surface which provides extra grip. Front shoes have one 'toe clip'.

The hind shoe, like the pony's foot, is not nearly so round as the front one. This shoe has two 'quarter clips', which are better for bigger ponies or those who do much jumping. They do much less damage than a toe clip if your pony is inclined to overreach (see 'Common Injuries').

The road shoe is also fullered, but it is not concave — both surfaces are the same width. Road shoes are too heavy for everyday use and give very little grip on grass, especially for cantering or jumping, or on hills. However, they can be useful for long journeys, such as treks, particularly on metalled roads. If you are going on a Pony Club trek, ask advice about this.

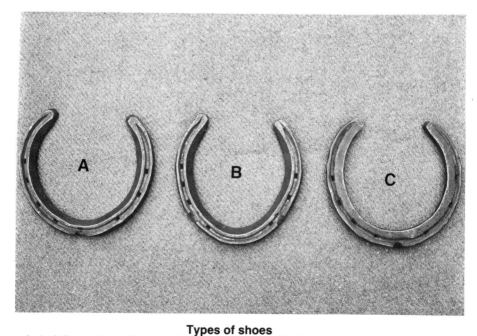

Types of shoes
A: Left front shoe. Concave, fullered, with pencilled heels. B: Left hind shoe, with quarter clips. C: Left front road shoe, fullered, but not concave. Note square heels.

SYSTEMS OF SHOEING

There are two systems of shoeing — hot shoeing and cold shoeing. In hot shoeing the shoes are specially made and fitted to the pony's foot while still hot, so that they can be adjusted before being cooled and nailed on. This is by far the most satisfactory method, but it means you will have to take your pony to the blacksmith, unless he has a portable forge. Cold shoeing is generally done with readymade shoes, and nothing like the same amount of adjustment is possible.

WHAT TO LOOK FOR WHEN THE PONY HAS JUST BEEN SHOD

1. That the right type and size of shoe has been used.
2. That the heels of the shoes are the right length. If too long, the shoes will be very easily pulled off; if too short, as the pony's feet begin to grow, the shoe may be pulled in on the corn place.
3. Any very high clenches, as the nail may have gone into the sensitive part of the foot (pricked foot) or close enough to press on it (nail binding). If there are high clenches, check carefully for soundness for the next few days and for signs of heat around the clench.
4. Any rasping round the wall of the foot. This removes the protective shiny coating and makes the foot brittle. If the wall has been rasped, be sure to oil the feet regularly.

It is always wise to have your pony shod about a week before anything such as a camp, course or trek, or a show or competition. Some ponies do go a little sore after shoeing, and this gives good time for the shoes to settle in, and to make sure that there are no problems such as pricks or nail binds.

The pony's foot is a wonderful thing, when you consider that this small area has to carry the entire weight of pony and rider. Often in jumping and galloping, all the weight is momentarily on one foot. It is not surprising that at least 75 per cent of lameness in ridden horses and ponies occurs in the foot.

Even if he is not actually lame, neglected feet will cause a pony much pain and discomfort; they may make him stumble and 'hit himself', and they will certainly prevent him from performing to the best of his ability. This is why daily inspection, including picking-out, and regular trimming every four to six weeks, are essential.

MEASUREMENT OF PONIES

Ponies are measured at the highest point of the withers.

Formerly, the standard unit of measurement was the hand, which is equivalent to four inches — approximately the width of a man's hand. With the introduction of metric measurements the centimetre became the standard unit. Since both are in general use, the following table will serve as a guide.

154

PONIES

CENTIMETRES	HANDS
102.5	10.0
105	10.1
107.5	10.2
110	10.3
112.5	11.0
115	11.1
117.5	11.2
120	11.3
122.5	12.0
125	12.1
127.5	12.2
130	12.3
132.5	13.0
135	13.1
137.5	13.2
140	13.3
142.5	14.0
145	14.1
147.5	14.2

HORSES

150	14.3
152.5	15.0
155	15.1
157.5	15.2
160	15.3
162.5	16.0

NOTE: 14.2 means 14 hands 2 inches, *not* 14 point 2 hands; and 14.2 hh means 14.2 hands high.

The measurement 147.5cm (14.2hh) is extremely important, as it marks the dividing line between a pony and a horse. There is no restriction in Pony Club events — your mount can be of any size, whatever your age — but in shows and jumping competitions under New Zealand Horse Society rules, ponies must not exceed 147.5cm. Similarly, for smaller ponies, the dividing lines are 137.5cm and 127.5cm.

This means that a pony that has no fault except that it is just too big for one particular class (130 or 140cm) or just over the 'pony' limit can often be bought much more cheaply than would otherwise be the case.

Life Measurement Certificates are issued by the Royal Agricultural Society of New Zealand. To obtain a life certificate, a pony must be not less than seven years old, and must be measured by an official using a Metcalfe Measuring Stand.

TERMS APPLIED TO PONIES AT VARIOUS AGES

At birth, a foal. A male is a colt foal, a female a filly foal. The year after birth the youngster becomes a yearling, the next year a two-year-old, then a three-year-old and so on.

A colt is a male horse or pony up to three years old.

A filly is a female horse or pony up to three years old.

A stallion or entire is an uncastrated male.

A gelding is a castrated male, of any age.

A mare is a female of any age.

HOW TO DESCRIBE A PONY

'Marcus', a chestnut pony gelding, rising six years old, 137.5cm (13.2hh) without shoes. Star and stripe. Stockings both forelegs, sock left hind. Scar left fore pastern. Mane and tail on.

Colours

If there is any doubt about a pony's colour, the colour of the 'points' is the deciding factor — the muzzle, tips of the ears, mane and tail and lower part of the legs.

A black pony is black all over, including the muzzle, though he may have white markings on the head or legs.

A brown pony is dark brown or nearly black, with black or brown points.

A bay pony is of a lighter and more reddish shade than a 'brown' one, with black points.

A chestnut pony is a ginger or yellowish colour. The mane and tail may be similar to the coat colour or very much paler — called 'flaxen'. They are never black. Light, dark, liver and golden chestnuts are variations of this colour.

A grey pony has black and white hairs mixed. When black hairs predominate, he is an 'iron' grey, if white hairs predominate, a 'light' grey. A 'fleabitten' grey (usually an older pony) has dark hairs occurring in tufts on a white coat. It is not correct to describe a pony as 'white', even if he is! All grey ponies get lighter as they age.

A dun pony can vary from mousy colour to golden, with black points. There is usually a dark stripe along the back (called a 'list') and sometimes there are 'zebra' markings on the limbs.

A blue roan pony has a basic coat colour of black or dark brown with a sprinkling of white hairs, and black points.

A strawberry or chestnut roan has a basic colour of chestnut, with a sprinkling of white hairs, and generally a chestnut mane and tail.

A red or bay roan pony has a basic colour of bay, again sprinkled with white hairs, and black points.

A cream pony has a cream-coloured coat on unpigmented skin. His eyes often appear pinkish, due to lack of pigment.

A palomino pony is a golden colour, with flaxen mane and tail.

An Appaloosa is a spotted pony. If the spots are white on a dark background, he is called a 'snowflake' Appaloosa.

A piebald pony has large, irregular patches of black and white.

A skewbald pony has similar patches of white and any other colour but black.

A whole-coloured pony is one that is the same colour all over, with no white markings.

Head

A star is a white mark on the forehead.

A stripe is a narrow white mark down the face.

A blaze is a broad white mark down the face which extends over the bones of the nose, and usually stretches from eyes to muzzle.

A white face includes the forehead, round the eyes, the nose and part of the muzzle.

A snip is a white mark between the nostrils, in some cases extending into the nostrils.

A wall eye shows white or blue-white colouring, due to lack of pigment.

Legs

A stocking is a white leg, extending from the foot to knee or hock.

A sock involves the fetlock and possibly part of the cannon. Smaller white marks on the legs are referred to as white fetlock, pastern or coronet, as the case may be.

Ermine marks are black spots occurring on white.

12
HEALTH, AILMENTS, INJURIES: C CERTIFICATE

ALTHOUGH well-cared-for ponies are generally healthy, it must be remembered that animals cannot speak for themselves. Therefore, all pony owners should learn to read the signs which indicate good health or the onset of possible illness.

These are the signs of good and bad health:

GOOD	BAD
1. The pony alert and interested in what is going on around him.	Standing with drooping head and a 'tucked up' appearance, on his own, away from other ponies.
2. Round in condition, with ribs well covered.	Excessively fat (gross condition), or thin and ribby.
3. The coat in summer should be sleek and glossy, though an unclipped pony in winter will naturally look shaggy.	Coat harsh or 'staring' — standing up on end instead of lying flat.
4. The skin should be loose, moving easily under one's hand.	Skin tight or 'hidebound' — often a sign of worms.

5. The eye bright and wide open (unless the pony is asleep!). The lining of the eye and nostril should be a deep salmon pink.

   Eye dull or half shut. Lining of eye and nostril very pale, yellow or bluish in colour. Discharge from eyes or nostrils.

6. Ears should feel warm — they are a good indication of whether the pony is warm enough all over.

   Ears cold and clammy.

7. Lower leg, below the knee and hock, should feel cool and 'fine', with tendons and ligaments standing out like hard cords.

   Legs hot and puffy or swollen. If one leg is affected, check carefully for lameness. If all four legs are 'filled' it could be due to a sudden change of diet, or to the pony eating something that has disagreed with him.

8. Feet should also feel cool. Frog should be firm but elastic, sole clean and hard.

   Any heat in the feet. Softness or a smelly discharge from sole or frog.

9. The pony should move 'sound', with a perfectly level, even stride.

   Any shortness or unevenness of stride. It is normal for a pony to 'rest' one hind leg, but not to 'point' or rest a foreleg while standing square on the other three legs.

10. Lying down for short periods and rolling occasionally, especially after work.

    Lying down for several hours on end. Rolling continually is often a sign of colic.

11. Breathing should be quiet, regular and rather slow, when the pony is at rest.

    Breathing that is quick, noisy or in any way laboured.

12. A hearty appetite.

    Not grazing for long periods. Refusing food.

13. Droppings — about eight piles should be produced daily. Colour will vary according to diet. They should just break on hitting the ground.	Hard, very dark droppings (constipated). Very loose with a pungent smell (diarrhoea).
14. Urine should be passed two or three times daily. It should be fairly thick, and light in colour.	Dark coloured urine. If a pony has difficulty in 'staling' — passing urine — this should be reported at once.
15. The pony going willingly and appearing to enjoy his work.	An unhealthy pony asked to work may appear crabby and lazy — just as you would!

Most of these signs of health may seem obvious, but it takes practice to notice the details quickly. If a pony is off-colour he should receive every attention as soon as possible. Seek assistance to find out the cause of the trouble, and carry out instructions carefully.

LAMENESS

Considerable experience may be needed to find the cause of lameness. The obvious signs are:

1. In acute lameness, the pony may move only with difficulty.

2. The stride will appear uneven. You may see, feel or hear it more easily if you trot him slowly on a hard surface.

3. The pony may nod his head towards the sound leg as it comes down, trying to keep his weight off the sore one.

4. He may 'rest' the leg if it is a hind one, or 'point' if it is a foreleg, or constantly shift from one leg to the other.

5. There may be heat or swelling in the affected leg — you should notice this while grooming. If there is heat or swelling in a leg, on no account should the pony be ridden until the cause has been found, even if he is not lame at the moment.

Note: It is correct to speak of a pony being 'lame' or 'sore', never 'limping'.

Never ride a pony you think is lame. Seek advice as soon as possible. If the pony goes lame while you are out riding, dismount and check his feet for a wedged stone, which must be removed at once, or for anything picked up in the feet, such as glass or a nail. Lead the pony home, or until he seems sound.

160

WOUNDS

There are three types of wounds:
1. Cuts — ranging from small scratches to deep wounds caused by wire, glass, etc.
2. Contusions — e.g. a kick.
3. Puncture — from thorns, stakes, nails, wire.
   With all wounds, first aid is important.

Small Cuts And Scratches

These should be noticed during your daily check in the paddock, or while grooming. They should not be neglected, or they may become infected.
1. Clean the wound by trickling the hosepipe over it (hold the nozzle a few centimetres above, don't squirt directly into the wound) or wash with cold water and salt (1 teaspoonful to ½ litre). If very dirty, Savlon or a similar mild lotion may be used. Follow the directions on the bottle, do *not* make it stronger than recommended.
2. Treat with antibiotic powder. Leave uncovered unless liable to become dirty, or to attract flies.
3. Check and treat daily. Do not wash after the initial cleaning.

Torn Cuts And Deeper Wounds

Cuts always bleed, sometimes severely, and this can be frightening, especially if you are on your own. As long as you keep calm and act quickly, you have every chance of dealing with the situation successfully. Apply direct pressure. Any material folded into a pad and pressed firmly against the wound — a handkerchief or even the heel of your hand will do. Don't worry if the blood seeps through the material — keep up the pressure for at least five minutes before checking. If possible, bandage the pad on to keep it in place. Having controlled the bleeding, try to get help and advice for further treatment.

Don't wash a deep wound that has bled freely, for the following reasons:
1. You may re-start the bleeding.
2. It could make the wound impossible to stitch, should this be necessary. If there is any question of stitching, the sooner the vet arrives the better. Even twelve hours may be too long if it starts to swell.

Contusions

Ponies sometimes kick one another and, when shod, can cause considerable damage. Even if there is no cut, there is always a bruise,

161

and often internal bleeding, so this type of injury can be very painful. If the skin is broken, infection is very likely and can spread rapidly in the contused area — in fact, an abscess can occur even when the skin is not broken.

If the kick is anywhere near a joint or on a bony part, keep the pony still and get veterinary assistance.

Otherwise, first apply a cloth wrung out in warm water, for about five minutes, then trickle the hosepipe over the area of the injury. Alternate warm and cold until the soreness and swelling are relieved. Treat the wound, if any, with antibiotic powder.

Punctures

The most dangerous type of wound. The surface injury is often so small that it may be overlooked, and it is impossible to know how bad the damage is underneath.

If near a joint or in the foot, veterinary assistance is essential. In some cases a poultice may be necessary — the vet will tell you how to apply this.

Otherwise, bathe with mild antiseptic and warm water at least twice daily, to soften the area and keep the wound open. Treat with antibiotic ointment from the vet. Do not use powder, as this will dry the surface of the wound too quickly.

It is essential that puncture wounds should heal from underneath, so that infection will not be trapped inside. If the wound starts to swell, or becomes hot and/or painful, call the vet at once. Tetanus is always a risk with this type of wound.

Tetanus (Lockjaw). Extremely painful and lethal. The germs are more likely to thrive in the enclosed conditions provided by small scratches and punctures than in larger and more open wounds.

It is strongly recommended that all ponies and horses should be immunised against tetanus. This is done by injection, with a follow-up at a later date, just as riders themselves should be immunised.

POOR CONDITION

Some of the principal causes of poor condition in ponies are:
1. Insufficient food.
2. Incorrect feeding. See 'Feeding' (page 128).
3. Mineral imbalance.
4. Internal parasites — worms and bots.
5. Teeth needing attention.

Worms

All ponies need regular dosing for worms. If the pony lives on a farm and grazes with other stock, twice a year may suffice. If he shares grazing only with other ponies, or lives on his own, particularly in a small paddock, he will need worming every six to eight weeks. A pony with a heavy worm infestation will not look, feel or go well, and may even die.

We will not go into the various types of worms at this stage, except to mention that the blood worms, which circulate in the bloodstream, are the most dangerous.

Symptoms of worm infestation. The coat may be hard, tight and staring. The pony will lose condition, he may be ribby and pot-bellied. He may rub his tail. The gums are often pale, with a bluish tinge. The pony may appear listless and tire easily. In some cases there may be a cough.

Treatment. Consult your vet on the best preparation to use. There are several available in powder or paste form, and most of them can be administered quite easily with assistance from an older person.

Regular dosing for worms is of the utmost importance, especially for ponies who live in small paddocks either alone or with others.

Bots

During the summer months the bot fly lays eggs on ponies' legs, on the lower parts of their bodies and in their manes. Be sure to remove these eggs during the daily grooming, otherwise the pony will lick them off and swallow them, thereby becoming infested with the bots' larvae.

Symptoms. As for worms. In bad cases the pony may be reluctant to stand still, stepping backwards and appearing slightly 'colicky'. He will tire very quickly when worked.

Treatment. Dose in mid-summer, and again in the autumn, about two weeks after the bot flies have disappeared. Consult your vet about suitable treatment. Medications combining worm and bot treatment are available. Occasionally it is necessary for the vet to dose the pony by putting a tube up a nostril into the stomach.

TEETH

Ponies have two sets of teeth. The sharp front ones are called 'incisors' and are used to bite the grass off. The back teeth, called 'molars', are used to chew the food thoroughly so that it can be digested. In ponies over the age of about six, these molars often develop sharp edges which make it uncomfortable, even painful, to chew properly. This means that either the pony will not eat enough, or that, because it is not chewed sufficiently, the food he does eat will not be well digested.

Symptoms. The pony quickly loses interest in hay, especially hard hay or lucerne. He dribbles half-chewed food out while eating. He doesn't appear to be 'doing' well for the amount of food he is receiving.

It may be possible to feel sharp edges by running your fingers along the outside of the cheeks. *Don't* try to open the mouth and feel from the inside, for obvious reasons!

Treatment. Have the teeth checked regularly. Autumn, at bot-dosing time, is best, so that the teeth will be in good order to deal with the winter's hay or hard feed. The vet will use a rasp to file off the sharp edges.

Younger ponies often have temporary teething problems when they are losing their milk teeth and the permanent ones are coming through. If the pony suddenly starts to throw his head about when ridden, and there is obvious soreness and inflammation in the gums, it may be necessary to use a rubber bit, or even to stop riding him altogether until the soreness disappears.

COLIC

Intestinal pain. Causes: Sudden change of diet, such as from grass to dry food, or on to rich pasture. Pony raiding the feed-room. Drinking too much water when hot. Drinking sandy water. Internal problems — worms, bots, indigestion, poisoning.

Symptoms. Pony looking round at his stomach, often kicking at it. Moving about restlessly, lying down and getting up again, pawing the ground. In more severe cases, rolling or thrashing about violently, grunting or sweating in patches (signs of pain).

Treatment. Keep the pony warm and lead him around quietly. He may be allowed to lie down if he is quiet, but if he tries to roll, get him up and moving at once. Violent rolling may result in a twisted gut.

If the symptoms are severe, or persist for longer than an hour, call the vet immediately. Failure to do so could be fatal. If you have to leave the pony to go for help, return to him as quickly as possible. A pony with colic should not be left alone, in case he has a sudden spasm.

LAMINITIS

Also called 'founder'. A very painful condition which affects the feet of ponies, and sometimes of horses.
Causes:
1. Overeating, especially when the grass is very rich in the spring. Too much heating food — e.g. grains such as oats, barley, or maize.

2. Sudden hard work when fat and unfit — e.g. a gallop along the beach on an unfit pony.
3. Fast work on hard ground.
4. A long drink of water when hot.
5. Neglect of the feet.
6. Grossly fat condition over a long period.

As a result of any of the above causes, the blood supply to the feet may be suddenly increased. Because of its hard wall, the foot cannot swell, and the pony will be in great pain. In severe cases, permanent damage to the foot may result.

Symptoms. Laminitis usually affects the front feet. The pony will stand with his hind feet stretched forward under him, to take as much weight as possible, and his forefeet pushed out in front, resting on the heels. He will be unwilling to move. The feet will feel warm, and the pony may be blowing or sweating.

Treatment. Send for the vet at once. Hosing the feet or putting ice packs on them will help to relieve the pain until he arrives, and may even prevent permanent unsoundness developing.

Obviously, prevention is the best policy. Take special care to keep ponies off lush spring paddocks, and bear in mind the other causes of laminitis. Even if there is no lasting disability from the first attack, the pony will always be more liable to founder in the future.

GRASS STAGGERS

Generally caused by a fungus which develops on ryegrass or paspalum. It occurs in late summer and autumn, especially in moist, humid conditions following a long dry spell. Certain paddocks may be worse than others, and some ponies are more prone to staggers than others.

Symptoms. The first sign is increased nervousness or jumpiness, even in a pony who is normally calm and quiet. In the next stage, he will be shivering or trembling, stiff and unco-ordinated in his movements. In bad cases, he may actually stagger, or even fall down and be unable to get up.

Treatment. Remove the pony from the paddock at once and keep him in a yard. Feed hay and bran mashes to avoid constipation due to the change of diet. See that he has plenty of water. It is essential to avoid all stress or excitement, and the pony should be disturbed as little as possible. If he has a companion and gets upset when separated, bring his mate in, too.

Close observation and prompt action at the initial, nervous stage should prevent the attack from becoming severe. Seek advice from experienced people locally or from your vet on when it is safe to return the pony to his paddock.

COUGHS

Causes: Virus infection from another pony, bronchitis, worms, choking, dust. It is best to get help to determine the cause as soon as possible. The sooner treatment starts, the easier it will be to clear the cough up.

Treatment. Keep the pony warm, dampen all feed, especially hay, don't ride him without veterinary advice and isolate him from other ponies.

COLDS

Causes: Virus infection from another pony, tying up in a cold or draughty spot when hot.

The first sign is a runny nose — the discharge is usually yellow and rather thick. There may or may not be a cough. Although colds are fairly common, they should not be taken lightly, especially if the pony has a cough too. They can easily lead to serious problems, and can be the start of strangles (a dangerous disease, rather like mumps, which ponies are subject to).

Treatment. As for coughs. Clean the nose thoroughly with damp cotton wool at least twice daily. The cotton wool should go straight into the rubbish bag. A little Vicks may be smeared round the nostrils, but not pushed up into the sensitive part of the nose. Should the pony appear dull, or his breathing become noisy or rapid, seek veterinary advice at once.

LICE

These small, whitish, blood-sucking and biting insects usually appear in the winter months, and can quickly cause a pony to lose condition. They are found mainly in the roots of the mane, along the neck, back and tail. In bad cases there may be bare patches caused by irritation and the pony rubbing himself. Heavy scurf will be found, particularly in the mane and tail, and on closer inspection the insects themselves will be seen.

Treatment. Use one of the proprietary brands of animal louse powder. The lining of the cover must also be powdered. Repeat the treatment in 17-21 days, to catch any newly-hatched lice. Isolate the pony and everything that is used on him (see page 168).

TICKS

Most of the 'ticks' found on horses are actually a form of blood-sucking louse — not to be confused with the winter type mentioned above.

Ticks may be found during the summer months on the pony's neck and body — usually in small numbers. The head is buried in the pony's skin and, as the insect's body fills with blood, it becomes very obvious. It is tempting to try to pull it off, but this may result in the head being left behind, causing infection.

Treatment. Louse powder is effective, or a wash may be obtained from the vet. Follow the directions carefully, as ponies' skins are very sensitive and if the wash is too strong it may irritate.

On no account use the 'pour-on' preparations that are made for treating lice or ticks in cattle; they can be fatal for ponies and horses.

RINGWORM

This is a highly contagious skin disease, caused by a fungus. It can easily be caught from other ponies.

Symptoms. Small, raised, circular patches of hair appear — about the size of a twenty-cent piece. Then the hair falls out and, if not treated, the patch will quickly extend. It usually starts on the neck and back.

Treatment. Iodine, Equidine, or gentian violet gently scrubbed in with an old toothbrush, two or three times weekly. Isolate the pony, and keep his grooming kit, saddlery, covers, *everything* that is used on him, away from others. Ringworm can be transmitted to people, so wash your hands thoroughly immediately after any contact with an affected pony.

MEDICINE CHEST

Most treatment by pony owners consists of first aid. This is why it is important to have a few simple things ready to use at once. By the time the shops open it may be too late.

Keep the following in a closed box or small suitcase:
1. Two small packets of cotton wool in polythene bags. (A big packet soon becomes dirty, once opened.)
2. Two 10 cm elastic bandages.
3. A bottle each of Equidine, Savlon, Triocel or similar remedies, witch hazel or methylated spirits.
4. A puff pack of antibiotic powder, from your vet.
5. A small packet each of epsom salts and common salt.
6. Zinc ointment.
7. A veterinary thermometer (to be used only by an adult).
8. Filta-bac or Coppertone Shade (for pink-nosed ponies).
9. If you live a long way from veterinary assistance, include colic drinks and eye ointment, from your vet.

CARE OF THE SICK OR INJURED PONY

At this stage it would be foolish for you to try to manage on your own. Naturally, you will want to do everything possible for your pony, and good nursing can do much to ease pain and hasten recovery.

The first and most important rule is to follow your vet's instructions exactly. There is no point in having him give his expert opinion if you then take the advice of all sorts of unqualified people. If the treatment prescribed does not appear to be working, or you are unsure about anything, contact the vet at once, just as you would a doctor.

Sick ponies generally like quiet company, particularly if they are alone and perhaps have to be confined in a yard or small paddock. Visit your pony regularly, not only to check on his condition, but just to be with him for a while. A quick brush over, sponging his eyes, nose and dock and picking out his feet will all help to freshen him up and make him feel wanted. Make sure he is warm enough, has shelter, and water within easy reach. If his appetite is poor, tempt him with his favourite food to keep up his energy and morale.

ISOLATION

This is essential for anything infectious, such as coughs and colds, or contagious (spread by touch) such as lice and ringworm. The following are the most important points when a pony has to be isolated:

1. The pony must be kept right away from others — just the other side of a fence is obviously of no use!
2. None of his equipment must be used by other ponies until it has been thoroughly cleaned and disinfected. Grooming kit especially should not be interchanged.
3. All feed boxes, haynets, buckets used by the affected pony must be kept for him alone, and not used by others.
4. The pony must be kept at home. He must *never* be taken to Pony Club, shows, or out hunting.
5. It follows that he should not travel in a float. If for some reason he has to travel, the float must be thoroughly disinfected immediately afterwards.
6. Wherever possible, the same person should attend the pony throughout. It is particularly important, if there are other ponies to attend to, that an overall, which can be taken off on leaving the isolation area, should be worn. Hands should be washed before handling others. If the pony is yarded or boxed, gumboots should be worn and a bath of disinfectant kept outside to step in before approaching other ponies.

Isolation is not easy but, properly carried out, it can be completely effective in preventing the spread of disease.

A reminder: the use of water troughs at shows is a dangerous practice — much infection is passed on in this way. Take your own bucket and fill from a tap.

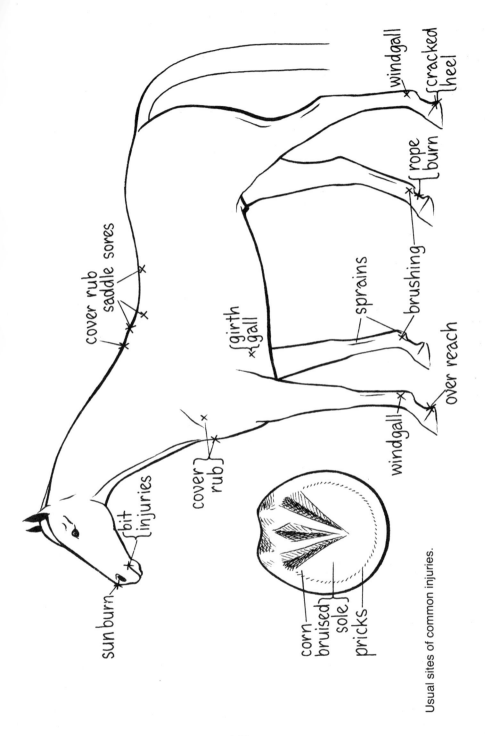

windgall

cracked heel

rope burn

cover rub
saddle sores

brushing

sprains

girth gall

over reach

bit injuries

cover rub

windgall

sun burn

corn
bruised sole
pricks

Usual sites of common injuries.

COMMON INJURIES

Class A. These injuries should be examined as soon as possible by an experienced person — e.g. your Pony Club instructor; an A or H Certificate holder, or somebody recommended by your instructor. If an experienced person is not immediately available, then consult your veterinary surgeon without delay.

INJURY	SYMPTOMS	CAUSES	TREATMENT
Eye	Eye running, closed or half-closed. Swollen.	Chaff etc. in eye. Blow or knock.	Get help at once. Keep pony in shade. Do *not* poke about in the eye.
Pricked foot	Lameness. Heat in foot.	A nail too high or inaccurately driven when being shod. Picking up a nail.	Get help at once. Anti-tetanus injection essential if not immunised.
Corns	Lameness, often intermittent. Heat in foot.	Leaving shoes on too long. Bad shoeing.	Usually discovered by the blacksmith during shoeing, in which case he will deal with them. Otherwise, if pony seems rather sore and 'pottery', seek advice. Once started, corns are liable to recur.
Bruised sole	As for pricks.	Treading on stones. Don't exceed walking pace on rough, stony surfaces.	Rest, stand in cold water if possible. If not better in two days, seek advice. If neglected, can be very painful and take a long time to heal.
Over-reach	A bruised wound on the heel or back of the fetlock of a foreleg, from the toe of the hind foot.	Jumping and galloping in heavy going. Hind toes too long. Sharp toe-clips on hind shoes.	If deep, the flap of skin may have to be cut off, by the vet. and anti-tetanus and antibiotic injections needed. Otherwise, keep as clean and dry as possible and treat with antibiotic powder. If it happens often, use over-reach boots and try to have pony shod with quarter-clips behind (see *Manual No. 2*).
Sprains	Lameness, heat, pain, general swelling.	Sudden stop or twist. Putting foot in hole. Too heavy rider. Hard work when unfit.	Rest is essential. Bathe with warm water, then cold, alternately, or hosepipe to relieve pain until help arrives.

Class B. These injuries should respond to the treatment suggested, but should be checked from time to time by an experienced person — as Class A — to make sure that all is going well. If in doubt at any time, *ask advice.*

INJURY	SYMPTOMS	CAUSES	TREATMENT
Sunburn	Nose pimply or scabby. Inflamed and painful.	Pink nose (lack of hair) exposed to sun. Lack of attention by owner.	Apply Filta-bac, or a similar barrier cream for horses, or a human suntan lotion such as Coppertone Shade. Prevention best.
Bit injuries	Sore corners of the lips or bars of mouth — the stretch of bare gum, between the incisor and molar teeth, where the bit lies.	Thin, rough or badly-fitting bit. Unfit, excitable pony. Rough hands.	Apply zinc ointment to lips. Keep bit out of mouth until healed. Use rubber or thick metal bit. Check fitting. Educate hands and pony.
Saddle sores	Raised patches of hair, soreness. Will become raw if neglected.	Poor grooming (dirt and sweat left in coat).	Always check when brushing out saddle mark. Bathe with witch hazel or methylated spirit. If raw, bathe with saline solution, apply zinc ointment. Don't ride until healed.
		Ill-fitting saddle.	Check fitting and soundness of saddle. Use sheepskin numnah or folded blanket as a temporary measure.
		Lazy, slouching rider. Unfit pony.	Smarten rider.
		Hot back left uncovered — called a 'scalded' back.	Keep back covered until cool.
Girth galls	Raised, sticky patches, soon becoming raw if neglected. Soreness.	Poor grooming. Unfit pony. Girth too hard/loose/tight.	Check when brushing out — do it thoroughly! Treat as for saddle sores. Pony may be ridden bareback. Use string girth. Check tightness.
Cover rubs	Bare, then raw, areas on wither, shoulders or chest.	Cover too big/small. Badly made, left on too long.	As for saddle sores. Check fitting. Sew in lambskin to cover top seam, front buckle. Check gusset for shoulder fit.

INJURY	SYMPTOMS	CAUSES	TREATMENT
Rope burns	Sticky, raw, painful patches behind hind pasterns. Pony may be lame.	Rope too long when tying up. Leg roping.	Wash with warm water and a mild antiseptic, such as Savlon, dry carefully. Apply Burnol or similar cream daily.
Cracked heels	Inflamed, sticky or scabby behind pastern. Pony may be lame.	Washing with warm water, and not drying. Brushing wet mud. Constant standing in deep mud.	Treat as for rope burns. If scabby, first wash with warm water and mild antiseptic, gently remove scabs, dry thoroughly.
Brushing	A bruise and/or cut on fetlock, from the shoe of the opposite foot.	Bad shoeing — shoes too heavy, badly fitting. Weakness in a young, old or poorly conditioned pony. Faulty action.	Check shoes, treat wound in usual way. Use brushing boots (see *Manual No. 2*). If due to weakness, check feeding, give steady exercise to build up condition.
Windgalls	Soft, puffy swellings around fetlock joint.	Too much work on hard ground, especially galloping about and jumping.	Go easy on fast work and jumping until ground softens. Hosepipe, holding hose about 1.5m away, fair pressure, for 5 minutes daily after work.

PART IV

SADDLERY AND EQUIPMENT

13
WHAT YOU NEED AND HOW TO USE IT — C CERTIFICATE

REQUIREMENTS FOR THE PONY

Halter (or head-collar)

Leather or rawhide is preferable to nylon, especially if the halter is to be left on in the paddock. Nylon is unbreakable if the pony gets caught up.

A good type of halter. The three buckles allow ample scope for adjustment. The heavy rope has a strong clip spliced on at one end only.

Rope

Should be heavy, approximately 15mm in thickness, 1.5 to 1.8 metres in length. Hemp or cotton is safer than nylon. Thin nylon is most dangerous if fingers get caught up in it.

A halter and lead-rope is essential for catching and tying up. Neither should be done with a bridle, as this would involve considerable risk of damage both to the bridle and the pony's mouth.

Bridle

The parts of a bridle are shown on this page, and different types of bridles on page 177. Plain, brown leather bridles are by far the best. The bit may be attached by either studs or buckles. Studs are neater, but more expensive and harder to undo.

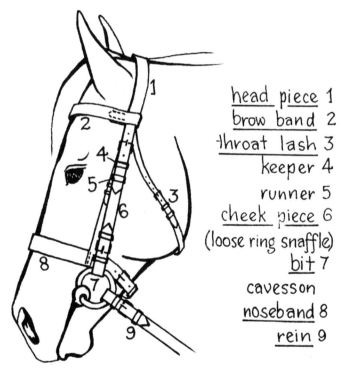

head piece 1
brow band 2
throat lash 3
keeper 4
runner 5
cheek piece 6
(loose ring snaffle)
bit 7
cavesson
noseband 8
rein 9

Parts of the bridle. D Certificate must know the ones underlined.

Bit

It is strongly recommended that you should ride your pony in a snaffle bit, with a drop noseband if needed — see page 177 However, there are many different kinds of snaffles, so it is important to know which one you are using, and how it works in the pony's mouth. A

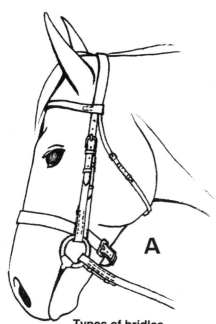

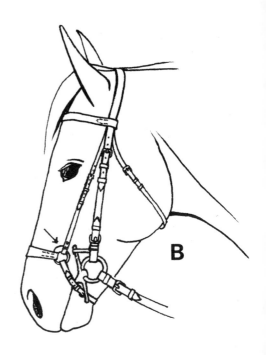

Types of bridles

A: *Split head,* where the head-piece and throat-lash are made from one piece of leather. Eggbutt snaffle is attached by studs, correctly turned inwards. Cavesson noseband. A smart and practical bridle, though more expensive than the other two.

B: *Loose head.* The throat-lash is separate, and is liable to get lost. It should be threaded through from right to left, underneath the head-piece. Note — keepers from the cheekpiece of the bridle to the cheek of the Fulmer bit and buckle attachments, correctly turned outwards.

Dropped noseband. Note small leather attachment from cheekpiece to front of noseband, to prevent it slipping down on the pony's nostrils.

C: Queensland or farm bridle. Usually too big for ponies, as shown here.

useful range of snaffles is shown on this page, together with some other bits, which should only be used on the recommendation of your instructor.

Action of bits. The thicker the bit, the milder it is. Ponies often pull through fear or pain, and will go better in a milder bit. The aim in selecting a bit is to find one that the pony respects and responds to, without being frightened of it. Whatever bit is used, it is the training and the rider's hands that make or mar the pony. Put very simply, bits act as follows:

Half-moon snaffles. Mild. Act on the tongue and corners of the mouth.

Jointed snaffles. Mild to severe, depending on thickness. They have a nutcracker, or squeezing, action on the bars and corners of the mouth.

Curb bits, including Pelhams and Kimblewicks. Fairly severe to cruel, depending on length of cheeks and tightness of curb-chain, which acts on the sensitive chin groove. The severity of these bits also depends on the rider's hands and temper. The jointed Pelham combines nutcracker and curb actions, and is not recommended.

No bit can act properly unless it is the right size for the pony and correctly fitted. Check frequently for sharp edges which could pinch the pony's lips.

For further details of the action of bits, including the double bridle, see the *Pony Club Manual No. 2*.

Bits

A: Rubber half-moon (or mullen-mouth) snaffle. The mildest bit available — often too mild, so that the pony doesn't respect it. Good for ponies who are frightened of the bit — possibly owing to their rider's hard or unsteady hands.

B: Metal half-moon snaffle. The next mildest bit. Also good for scared ponies suffering from bad hands, or for young ponies or those who play with the bit too much. Many ponies will in time begin to lean on half-moon bits, if used constantly, but these bits are useful for ponies who dislike the action of a jointed bit.

C: Jointed, loose-ring snaffle, cob size. A good thickness. Wire (round) rings are less likely to pinch the lips.

D: Jointed, loose-ring snaffle, pony size. A good bit, but the flat rings need a bigger hole, which may cause pinching.

E: Fulmer snaffle. The advantages of this bit are: it cannot pull through the pony's mouth, and the cheeks help in turning. The bit is very still in the pony's mouth, when used with keepers. It cannot pinch the lips. Never tie your pony up when he is wearing a Fulmer — the long cheeks could get caught up. Fulmers are not allowed for Polo-crosse and some other games.

F: Tom Thumb snaffle. Cannot pull through the mouth or pinch the lips. A good bit for small ponies: the shorter cheeks are less dangerous and Tom Thumbs are sometimes thicker than the same-sized plain snaffle.

G: Eggbutt snaffle. Cannot pinch the lips. The fixed rings allow less play than a loose-ring snaffle. Some ponies dislike this action, but if your pony goes happily in an eggbutt, don't change it.

H: Half-moon pelham.

I: Kimblewick.

J: Eggbutt snaffle. Very thick in the corners and thin at the joint. Can be uncomfortable if used with a dropped noseband.

K: Very thin loose-ring snaffle. Some older or stronger ponies go quite well in these, but they should not be used on ponies with light mouths, or on young ponies. Consult your instructor before using any of these last four bits. If you use a curb bit, you *must* learn to adjust the chain correctly.

L: Jointed pelham. Often seen in the showring. Not recommended.

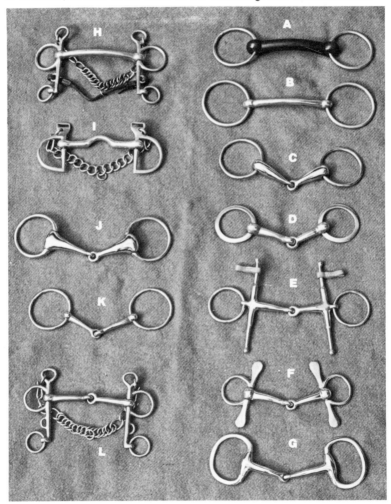

Reins

Leather, either plain or laced, is the best material. Reins should be approximately 1.3 metres long and 15mm wide for small ponies and riders. If too long, the loop is liable to catch round the rider's foot. There must be a firm buckle with a keeper. It is extremely dangerous if reins come undone when riding.

Rubber-covered reins are clumsy, though they can be useful in wet weather. Plaited cotton reins are easy to handle — nylon tends to be rather hard and to stretch.

Saddle

For the very young, a thick sheepskin, used wool side up, with surcingle and stirrups attached, is practical and cheap, and more comfortable than a felt pad.

For riders over the age of seven or eight a saddle, though expensive, should be obtained if you are riding for longer periods, or have got to the stage of going out and about with your pony. Riding bareback is not recommended as a regular thing — it leads to the bad habit of gripping with the back of your calf.

The most important things about a saddle are: (a) that it should fit both pony and rider, and (b) that its shape should assist the rider to sit correctly. A bad saddle can make this impossible.

A general-purpose saddle is the best at this stage. Its flaps are cut to allow the rider to shorten the stirrups for jumping, and the essential dip in the seat is in the centre (see photo on page 181).

Saddles which slope to the rear, flat saddles, racing exercise saddles, all lack this central dip and should be avoided. Stock-type saddles usually have a good central seat, and can be useful for older riders who are not so interested in jumping. The shape and length of the flaps make it difficult to shorten the stirrups for jumping.

All saddles, good or bad, are costly, even when bought second hand.

Never buy a saddle without trying it on your pony. Seek expert advice at this stage to make sure it is suitable and that it fits you both. Also, if it is secondhand, that it is in sound condition, especially the tree. Buying a saddle without these careful checks frequently results in great disappointment.

Numnah Or Saddle-cloth

Used to cushion pressure on a horse's back — e.g., a sheepskin — or, more usually with ponies, to protect the saddle lining. A numnah, cut to the shape of the saddle, is preferable. It should be attached to the girth-strap to keep it in place. You need two numnahs to allow for regular washing.

Sheepskin. Excellent for ponies with sensitive backs, but not too easy

Parts of the saddle. D Certificate candidates must know the ones underlined.

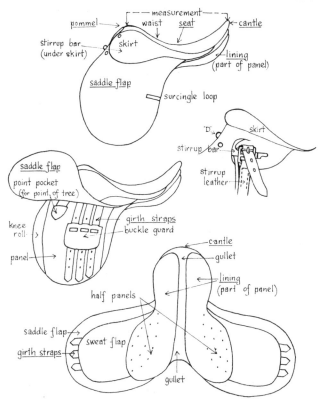

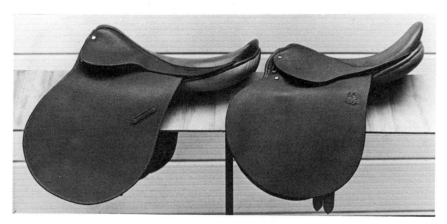

Bad and Good saddles
Left: The pommel is much higher than the cantle, and the lowest point of the seat is too far back. Right: The cantle is higher than the pommel, and the dip is in the centre. Flaps are cut a little forward, to allow for shortening stirrups for jumping. A good general-purpose saddle.

to keep clean. Use with woolly side to horse's back.

Felt. Good, but not so absorbent as sheepskin. Difficult to wash.

Wool or brushed nylon. Adequate and easy to wash.

Wool-covered foam rubber. Hot for the pony's back — difficult to wash.

Saddle-cloths. A carefully folded blanket will suffice, and can be useful to pack up an ill-fitting saddle but only as a temporary measure.

Towels tend to ruck up. They are unsightly as saddle-cloths and are best kept for drying the pony!

Stirrup-irons

Should be large (but not large enough for the rider's foot to slip right through), and heavy. Minimum clearance, 2cm when the foot is over to one side of the iron, which must be under the ball of the foot. The best material for stirrup-irons and for bits is stainless steel. The mixture metals such as eglantine or silverine are good, but pure nickel is too soft and can bend or snap. Check that the irons are still big enough every time you buy new boots. The picture below shows various types of stirrup-irons.

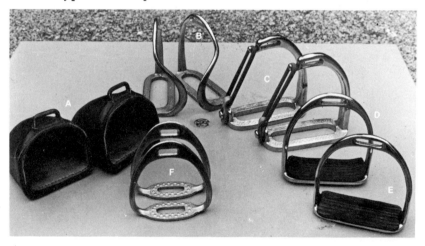

Stirrup-irons

A: Clogs. Only of use on a felt pad or sheepskin which has no safety bars. Otherwise not recommended as they encourage the rider to poke the toe down — a difficult habit to overcome later.

B: Simplex stirrups. Intended as a safety iron, but not recommended as it is possible in a fall for the foot to get stuck in the bend of the iron.

C: Peacock stirrups. A safety iron, sometimes used for younger riders. Disadvantages — the rubber is easily lost; the studs may get caught up; and the weight of a heavier rider in mounting will, in time, pull them out of shape.

D: Plain, heavy irons, recommended for all, provided the saddle has safety

182

bars, and the size is correct. In (D) the rubber tread is too big, turning up at the ends. This is dangerous.

E: Treads are quite safe if correctly fitted, as in (E), and are recommended. They help the rider to keep the iron under the ball of the foot.

F: Cradle pattern racing irons, made of aluminium. Not recommended: they are too light and could be dangerous.

Stirrup Leathers

Should be of good quality and the correct width to fit the iron. Check that the buckle has a central groove to retain the tongue in position, that the stitching is sound and the holes level.

Girth

Various types of girths are shown in the picture below.

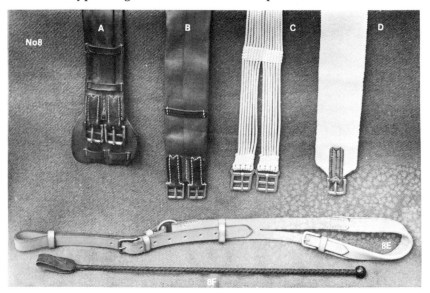

Types of girths

A: Short leather girth, with built-in buckle guard, for use with long girth straps.

B: Full-length leather girth. A good type of girth, provided it is looked after and kept soft. Expensive, but wears well.

C: Nylon-string girth. Good for ponies, especially those inclined to gall. Cheap and easily washable.

D: Webbing girth. The type shown should never be used on its own — it is not strong enough, has only one buckle and could cause girth galls. The tubular type, with two buckles, is better.

E: A crupper.   **F:** A good type of whip.

The Following May Be Needed:

Neckstrap. Essential in the early stages of riding and jumping. A martingale neckstrap or other strap round the pony's neck.

Surcingle. A narrow girth that goes over the top of the saddle. Not generally necessary with a sound saddle and a good two-buckle girth. If it must be used, check that the skirt of the saddle is not held down, preventing the stirrup leather coming off in an emergency.

Crupper. Useful if the saddle tends to slip forward, especially on hilly country. Goes under the tail, and is attached to a special dee at the back of the saddle. Check that this dee doesn't press on the pony's spine. Picture on page 183.

Breastplate — to prevent the saddle slipping back. Breastplates require careful fitting — if you think one may be needed, ask advice.

Martingale. Standing and running martingales are shown on page 185. A standing martingale consists of a neckstrap and another strap which goes through the neckstrap and is attached to the girth at one end and the noseband at the other. It must *only* be attached to a cavesson noseband. A running martingale has rings through which the reins pass. Ask advice before using any martingale.

Covers. Apart from ponies that are clipped, thoroughbred types or older ponies living in colder parts of the country, covers are not always necessary for ponies. They grow their own thick winter coats and, providing there is some shelter in the paddock, many ponies can cope very well without covers.

Covers are expensive; at least two will be needed to allow for changes in bad weather, and daily supervision is essential.

If a cover is used it must fit well and should not be too heavy — a wet cover trebles in weight and can be very restrictive.

Apart from warmth, a cover does help to keep a pony clean, but it must be taken off and the pony brushed over at least every other day, otherwise he may become itchy.

REQUIREMENTS FOR THE RIDER

1. **An Approved Helmet** complying with NZ Safety Standards 8602, Medium, not Lightweight Protection, 8601. British S4472, Australian S2063 or equivalent should always be worn when riding. It is compulsory for all Pony Club jumping activities, including practice. A hard cap (NZSS 2059) with leather or nylon strap, not elastic, is permissible for flat work.

Martingales

A: Standing martingale. When attached at both ends, the slack should easily reach up to the gullet, as the dotted line shows.

B: Running martingale. When attached to the girth with both rings up one side, these rings should reach within 10cm of where the neckstrap lies. Note stops on reins to prevent rings catching on the buckles. Both martingales have a rubber ring at the junction with the neckstrap to prevent the slack from hanging down between the pony's legs.

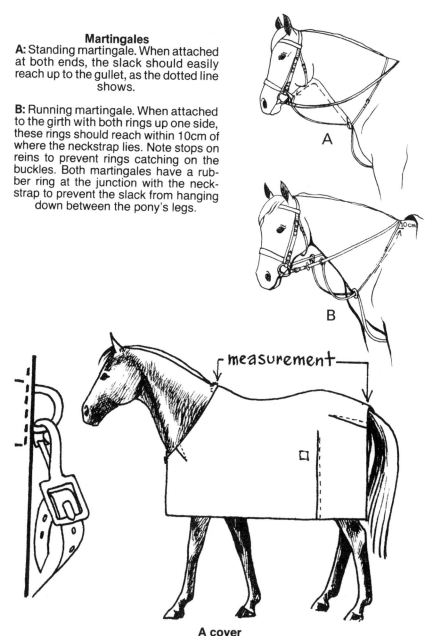

A cover

When buying a new cover allow for some shrinkage, as shown here. When worn in, it should just reach to the top of the tail. Note extra gussets to improve fitting. The clips on the leg straps should always be turned inwards, to avoid getting caught up on fences.

2. **Suitable Footwear.** Jodhpur boots are ideal — failing this, lace-up shoes with heels and smooth soles. Cleated gumboots, shoes without heels, with wedge heels or large buckles are all dangerous, as they can get wedged in the stirrup-iron. Uncleated gumboots are in order for small children. Long, black leather or rubber riding boots look very smart, but are not necessary for the younger rider. Fashion boots are a 'No-no' for everybody!

3. **Jodhpurs** are the neatest and most comfortable wear for riding, and prevent your knees from getting rubbed. They are part of the Pony Club uniform.

4. **The Top Half.** Any neat T-shirt or sweater is in order. Tank tops and sun-tops are unsuitable — apart from looking sloppy, they give no protection to the shoulders in the event of a fall. Pony Club uniform is usually a white shirt with tie or jersey in the club colour. Jackets are quite unnecessary in the early stages. If worn, a tweed jacket is much more practical than a black one, and is the correct thing to wear with jodhpurs. Earrings not allowed.

5. **A Raincoat.** A close-fitting parka or swandri type is best. Voluminous, flapping garments can startle the quietest pony at times.

6. **Whip.** A good type, with a knob at the top and a wide flapper at the bottom is shown (page 183). The whip should not have a loop to put your hand through; this can be dangerous if you fall off, and makes it difficult to use the whip correctly or to change it from one hand to the other. Long dressage whips are not recommended at this stage, and *never* for jumping, for which they are much too severe.

7. **Gloves.** Useful in wet weather, or when riding a strong pony. Plain leather or string are the best materials. Gloves should always be worn in turnout classes.

8. **Your Pony Club Badge.**

SADDLING, BRIDLING, COVERING

Saddling Up

1. Check "Care Of Pony Before And After Riding", pages 144–5. Leave the pony tied up after you have brushed him over. If cold and/or wet, throw his cover over loosely.

2. Fetch saddle and bridle. Have the girth attached on the right side and laid across the seat of the saddle. The stirrup-irons must be run up. If a numnah is used, attach it to the saddle. Undo the throat-lash of the bridle. The picture on page 187 shows how to carry the saddle and bridle. On returning to the pony, hang up the bridle on a fence post or peg, don't dump it in a heap on the ground.

3. Put on the saddle. If you use a saddle-cloth, lay this on the pony's back first, keeping it slightly forward. Make sure there are no rucks or

A workmanlike approach. Note the stirrups correctly run up — see page 21. Rein buckle on shoulder keeps reins off ground. A nice clean numnah!

wrinkles, and that it is not folded so that the weight will come on a fold or seam. Put the saddle firmly but gently on the back, also slightly forward of the place where it should sit, and slide saddle and cloth together back into position, fitting snugly just behind the pony's shoulders.

Never pull the saddle or cloth forward, which would leave the pony's hair ruffled up underneath. If you get them too far back, you must take them off and start again. Now slip under the pony's neck to the right side, and check that all is flat and smooth there. Let down the girth.

Return to the left side. Check again that the saddle-cloth or numnah is lying flat, push it well up into the front arch of the saddle — as shown below.

Take the girth and buckle it up fairly loosely, so that you can easily get the flat of your hand between the girth and the pony (picture, page 189). If your saddle has three girth straps, use the first two or the first and third, not the back two. If you use two webbing girths, the second one should be on top of the other, using the first two girth straps.

The numnah or saddle-cloth should be pushed up into the arch of the saddle so that it is well clear of the pony's withers.

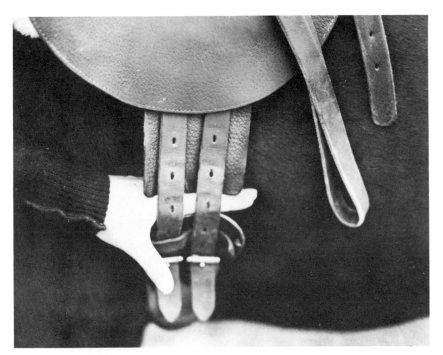

The girth should be no tighter than this when the saddle is first put on. Tightening it up at once encourages the pony to blow himself out or nip you.

It is best to put the saddle on first, because this gives it time to warm up and settle on the pony's back. Throw the cover over the saddle, if necessary.

Fitting of saddle. Although the fitting of your saddle will have been checked when you bought it, you will still need to re-check it frequently. The stuffing packs down with wear, and changes in the condition of the pony can also affect the fit of the saddle.

Looking from the front along the channel of the saddle, you should be able to see daylight quite clearly. This ensures that there will be no weight or pressure on the pony's spine. Pressure on any part of the spine could cause serious injury.

The commonest fault is for the saddle to come down on the wither. This is very painful for the pony, and dangerous. You should be able to get four fingers edgeways under the front arch of the saddle when unmounted, three fingers when you are in the saddle.

Check that the saddle is not pressing in behind the top of the shoulders, which would restrict their action.

If the saddle begins to come too close in front, a wither pad, made from a piece of foam rubber, or even a folded towel, may be pushed up into the front arch of the saddle, but only as a temporary measure.

Take it to the saddler before it reaches the stage of pressing on the wither or any other part of the pony's spine.

4. Put on the bridle. Check that the cheekpieces are level and at the correct length. Undo the noseband of the halter and slide the halter down the pony's neck, so that he is still tied up. Slip the reins over the pony's head — leave them lying with the buckle just in front of the wither. From here on there are two possible methods: Method A — shown in this picture.

Facing the same way as the pony, hold the headpiece of the bridle

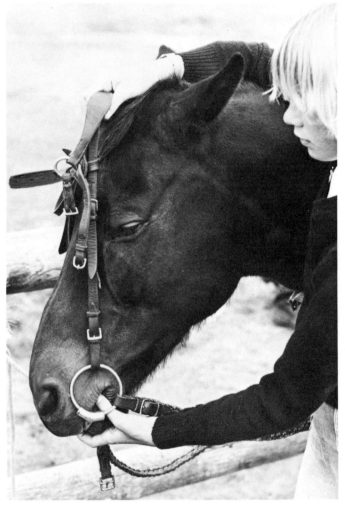

Putting on a bridle, *Method A.* If you are tall enough to reach, the arm over the pony's poll helps to control pony and bridle. Thumb opens mouth — no teeth here — and finger guides bit in.

190

and the front of the noseband in your right hand in front of the pony's forehead. Rest the bit on your left hand, ready to slide it into his mouth, as shown. Then draw the bridle up with your right hand, and slip the headpiece over his ears, letting the noseband drop down as you do so. Pull out the forelock, make sure the bridle fits comfortably behind his ears and the browband is straight.

In Method B you put your right hand under the pony's jaw and round over the top of his nose, just above the nostrils. Hold both cheekpieces in this hand, keeping it close to the pony's face. Your left hand opens his mouth and guides the bit in, as in Method A, and your right hand draws the bridle up.

Having got the bridle on, do up the throat-lash — you should just be able to turn your hand over between it and the pony's cheek bone.

5. Fitting of bit. Then check the fitting of the bit. A jointed snaffle should be high enough to make one small wrinkle in the corners of the mouth. If you take the bit on either side and hold it straight in the mouth, it should clear the lips by about 1cm on each side.

Next do up the noseband. A cavesson noseband must be inside the cheekpieces on *both* sides. It should be approximately halfway between the cheekbone and the corner of the pony's mouth, and you should be able to get two to three fingers edgeways between the front of the noseband and the pony's nose.

A dropped noseband goes underneath the bit — also on both sides. It must be well up on the bony part of the nose in front, but not so high that it pulls the bit too tightly into the corner of the mouth. It fits into the chin groove at the back. With this, you should be able to get two fingers in the front. *Note:* A dropped noseband must be used *only* with a snaffle bit — *never* with a Pelham or Kimblewick.

Finally, check that everything is straight, and that all keepers and runners are in place.

If you are going to leave the pony saddled up, always tie him up, so that he won't roll with the saddle on. This could break the tree. Secure the reins, so that he won't get them over his head and tread on them. The picture on page 192 shows a simple method of doing this if the reins are not long enough to slip behind the irons when they are run up.

When you are ready to mount, untie the pony and hang up the halter. Tighten the girth — run your fingers down to make sure that there are no wrinkles behind the elbows. Check that the buckle guards are pulled down over the buckles. You should now be able to slip two fingers under the girth. Untuck leathers from irons, which should be run down carefully to avoid scoring the leathers — right one first. Then put the reins over the pony's head, and up you get.

Unsaddling

On dismounting, immediately take the reins over the pony's head, run up the stirrups and slacken the girths a couple of holes.

1. Do up the headpiece of the halter round the pony's neck — leave the noseband undone. Tie him up.

2. Undo the noseband of the bridle, then the throat-lash. Put your left hand on the pony's nose, well above the nostrils, to steady his head, and slip the headpiece over his ears with your right hand. Bring the bridle down slowly, allowing the pony to ease the bit out of his mouth himself. If you snatch the bridle off quickly and roughly it will hurt his teeth, and naturally he won't be too keen on having it put on next time. Never take a bridle off with the noseband or curb chain done up.

3. Put the headpiece of the bridle with the reins over your left shoulder, slide the halter up the pony's neck and do up the noseband. Hang up the bridle while you take off the saddle.

4. Undo the girths, letting them go gently. Lift the saddle and slide it slightly back and towards you. Take the saddle in the crook of your left arm and, with your right hand, take the girth as it comes over the pony's back and lay it across the seat of the saddle. If it is muddy, turn it muddy side out, so that it won't scratch the saddle.

If the pony is sweaty under the saddle, slacken the girth another hole or two and ease the saddle on his back, but leave it on while you are attending to the rest of him — (see 'Care of the pony after Riding').

5. Put the saddle and bridle tidily away. Even if you are not going to clean them completely, *always* wash the bit as soon as possible after you take it out of the pony's mouth. It is much easier to clean while it is still wet, and you must never put a dirty bit into a pony's mouth. If the girth or saddle lining are muddy, you must remove the mud, otherwise it will give the pony girth galls and damage the saddle.

A pony is unlikely to get his foot in the reins if they are doubled round his neck like this.

Putting On A Cover

The pony must be tied up. If possible, lay the cover along the fence or gate and fold in half, bringing the back over the front. This will make it easier to handle for a smaller person, and is advisable if the pony is young or nervous.

Hold the front of the cover on either side of the centre seam and lift it carefully over the pony, so that it sits well forward. Unfold the back half and slide the cover back to within a few centimetres of normal position. Do up the leg straps. Having fastened the left strap, to the left D, the right strap is threaded through the left one before being secured to the right D. See that the clips are turned inwards, towards the pony, when fastened.

Lastly, do up the front strap. Never shift the cover forward once it is on, it ruffles the hair and is most uncomfortable.

Taking Off A Cover

The pony must be tied up. Undo the front strap and then, standing close beside the pony, not behind him, undo the leg straps one at a time, and secure at once. If necessary the front half of the cover may be folded back over the rear. Pull the cover off, sliding it back and towards you.

Note: Never have the cover on the pony with the front strap done up while the leg straps are undone. It could blow over the pony's head or fall round his front feet, possibly causing a serious accident.

CARE AND CLEANING OF SADDLERY

Good saddlery, or 'tack', is expensive, but it is well worth the money. Properly looked after, it will keep its value and will always be a credit to you and your pony. Neglected tack can cause bad accidents, and be most uncomfortable for the pony.

Never drop your saddle, leave it where the pony could step on it, or leave it on his back when he is not tied up and could roll on it.

Never leave a saddle sitting on the pony's back without a girth, or with the girth undone. Any fall or violent bump could break the tree — the framework on which the saddle is built. A saddle with a broken tree is quite useless and can seriously damage the pony's back.

If you have to put your saddle down anywhere, stand it on the front of the flaps, pommel down, and lean the cantle against a wall or post. Put your saddle-cloth or girth over the cantle to protect it.

Never put any tack down on a gritty surface.

Storage

Damp is one of the worst things for tack, so it should be kept in a reasonably cool, dry and airy place. Keep the saddle on a saddle-horse or a special bracket, and the bridle hung up by the headpiece —

Taking off a cover — easy and safe.

old saddle-soap tins nailed to the wall make excellent bridle-hangers. Tack must be kept well away from dust and vermin, such as rats and mice. A saddle-cover, not plastic, helps to protect the saddle.

Cleaning

Ideally, tack should be cleaned every day, but few people have time for this. If you have a new saddle or bridle it really must be cleaned every time you use it for the first few months, to help to 'break it in'. If your tack has got wet or muddy it should be cleaned as soon as possible after the ride. Otherwise, try to give your tack a quick rub over, without stripping it, every day it is used. It is surprising how little time this takes, and how effective it is. If you are riding daily, about once a week take it to pieces and give it a thorough clean.

Materials Required For Tack Cleaning

1. Saddle soap — either the glycerine bar-soap or the tinned variety.
2. A sponge or cloth for applying the soap.
3. A cloth for washing.
4. Metal polish if your bit and irons are nickel, but *not* if they are stainless steel.
5. A bucket of warm water.
6. A soft cloth for a final polish.

Method Of Cleaning

Strip the saddle — i.e. take off the irons and leathers, the girth and the buckle guards. Take the treads out of the irons, and put them all into the bucket of water to soak if they are muddy.

Dip your washing cloth into the water and wring it out thoroughly — it should be damp, not dripping wet. Stand the saddle on a smooth surface and wash the lining, if it is a leather-lined saddle. Use as little water as possible. Serge linings should be brushed or, if very dirty, scrubbed lightly with warm water. They must be thoroughly dried before use.

Now put the saddle on the saddle-horse and wash it, starting from the underneath and working outwards, first one side, then the other. Every scrap of grease and dirt must be removed before soaping. If there are black grease-spots — called 'jockey boys' — the best weapon to remove them is some hair from a pony's mane or tail. Make it into a hard pad by tying a series of knots, and damp it in your warm water. You can scrub as hard as you like with this, without any danger of scratching the leather.

Next dip the soap sponge in the water, and, again, wring it out thoroughly. Rub the sponge on the bar of soap, and soap the saddle all over, starting from underneath, as before. When you need more soap, it is best to dip the bar of soap into the water, rather than wetting the sponge again. If it lathers, it is too wet. Rub the soap in liberally, with a circular motion, particularly on the underneath of the flaps. Clean the buckle guards and stirrup leathers in the same way, and polish the irons with metal polish, unless they are stainless steel. Clean and dry the treads.

Girths. Leather girths are cleaned as above. They *must* be kept soft — if allowed to go hard, they will crack and/or give your pony girth galls. For the three-fold variety, it is a good idea to cut a piece of flannel or other woollen material to fit inside the girth, and keep this material soaked in oil. Use saddle soap on the outside.

String girths should be washed in soap and water and dried thoroughly before use.

Webbing girths should be brushed with a stiff brush and washed when necessary.

Cleaning the bridle. Take it to pieces. If the bit is dirty put it in the water to soak, then clean all leather-work as above. If you use metal polish on the bit, rinse it off before the final polish. When you put the bridle together make sure that the cheek pieces are level and in the right holes, and that you put the bit in the right way up. A jointed bit put in the wrong way round is extremely uncomfortable for the pony.

Oil. The gylcerine in the saddle-soap will keep leather soft in normal circumstances. Too much oil makes tack dirty, and will turn the leather black, instead of the rich mahogany colour that saddle-soap produces. It also rots the stitching, and can make the leather *too* soft and 'squidgey'. Oil is only needed to soften tack after it has had a real soaking, or for new leather. The best kinds to use are olive, castor or neatsfoot, never a mineral oil such as motor oil. After washing, rub the oil in thoroughly — don't use too much. Only oil the underneath of your saddle — it will soon soak through, but oil applied to the outside will spoil the colour of the saddle and make your clothes filthy. Allow time for the oil to soak in, and soap it before use.

New tack may be oiled lightly all over before you use it. Olive oil is probably best for this — in cold weather it should be slightly warmed. After this, clean and saddle-soap it daily. It may be necessary to give it one more oiling within a week or so, but this should be sufficient. Never again oil the seat or the outside of the saddle flaps.

Covers. Give the cover a good shake and air the lining regularly. Brush it to remove loose hair, especially when the pony is changing his coat. Oil front and leg straps to keep them soft. Waterproof them, especially along the top seam, every year. A leaking cover is far worse than no cover at all.

Checking Your Tack

Always check all stitching, runners and keepers, and buckles as you clean your tack. Give special attention to:

The saddle. The stuffing, to see that it is not becoming flat or lumpy. The lining, for cracks or signs of wear.

The girth straps. However strong your girth, you are still dependent on the webbing and stitching by which the girth straps are attached to the saddle. Give each one a good hard tug every time you clean the saddle. Check also that the holes are not running into one another.

Stirrup leathers. Check stitching. If you always mount from the left side, the left leather will stretch more than the right one, so change them over weekly.

The bridle. The bit, to see that it is not becoming sharp in the corners, or wearing thin at the joint.

Do — always get any necessary repairs done promptly. Apart from danger and discomfort to you and your pony, the longer you leave it, the bigger and more costly the job will be.

Don't — ever use very hot water, soda, detergents, wire-wool or a knife on your tack.

Don't — have your tack mended with rivets.

Don't — dry your tack in hot sun, or close to an open fire, or a radiator.

INDEX
Illustrations are shown in bold type,
(diagrams and/or photographs).

Age, terms to describe 156.
Aids,
  artificial 55
  for canter 31, 61
  for circles 59
  for transitions 26, 28, 29, 56, **57, 58,** 86, 103
  for turns 26, 58
  natural 55
Ailments 163-167
Arena, dressage 102

Back and seat, use of 45, 55
Barley 131
Best rider classes 97
Bits, types of 178-**9**
Bot
  eggs 126, 163
  knife **146**
Bots 113, 163

Bran 130
Bread 131
Breast-plates 184
Bridles,
  types of **177**
  care and cleaning 196
  fitting 191
  putting on **190,** 191
  taking off 192
Bruised sole 170
  wounds 161
Brush
  body 145, **146,** 148
  dandy 37, 145, **146**
  small (D Cert) 37, **146**
  water 145, **146**
Brushing **169,** 172
Bucking 116

Camps and treks 77

Canter
    aids 31, 61
    disunited 62
    leading leg 61
    position at **32**, 53
Care of pony 35, 43, 121
    before and after riding 144
    with change of seasons 126
    sick or injured pony 167
Carrots 131
Catching **35**
Cavalletti, construction **88**
    use **83**
Chaff 130
Change of pace 26, 28, 29, 31, 56,
    57, 58, 61, 86, 103
    rein 74
Circles, 58
    aids 59, **60, 61**
    twenty metre **75**
    use of whip in **60**
Clipping 149
Clips, belly **149**
    trace **150**
Clothing, rider's 184-6
Colds 166
Colic 164
Colour 156
Condition 113, 136, 162
Contagion 168
Corns **152**, 170
Coughs 166
Covers, care of 196
    fitting 184, **185**
    putting on 193
    taking off 193, **194**
Cross country 108-110
Crupper 184
Curry comb 37, 126, **146**, 148
Cuts 161

Dairy ration 130
Description of ponies 156, 157
Diagonals 53
Dismounting 20
Dressage 102-108

Exercise 102, 108, 139
Exercises for rider 29, 30, **31**, 49, **50**
Eye injuries 144, 170

Fat ponies 113, 127, 128, **136,** 165
F.E.I. 99, 100-101
Feed, types of 129-131
Feeding 128-140
    charts 140
    in paddocks 132
    rules 138

Fences, for paddock 123
Feet, care of 150-151
    picking up **147**
    picking out 38, 145, **147**
    structure **151**
First pony, buying a 12
Floats, loading, unloading 72, 142-3
Fording streams and rivers 71
Footwear 186
Founder 164
Frog 151
Galls, girth 77, 93, 116, 171
    saddle, 93, 116, 171
Gates, opening and shutting 68, **69**
    paddock 123
Girths, types of **183**
    cleaning 196
    fitting 188
    tightening **54, 189,** 191
Grass-kept pony, requirements of
    122, 136
Grooming
    kit **146**
    daily procedure 145-148
    for special occasions 148
Gymkhanas, training 94, **95,** 96-99

Halt, aids to 26, 56
Hand, metric 154
Handling 36, 141
Hands, use of 26, 47, 55
Hard feed 129, 132
Hay, good and bad 129
    feeding out 132
    nets and racks 132, **134**
Headgear 184
Health, signs of good and bad 158
Height 155
Hoof, structure of 150, **151**
Hoof pick **146, 147**
Horse,
    nuts or pellets 130
    points of a **34**
    trials 108-110
Hosing,
    as a grooming method, 149
    wounds 161
Hunting 77

Indigestion 164
Injuries 170-172
    sites of **169**
Isolation 168

Jumping
    equipment 79, **82, 86, 87**
    F.E.I. 99-101
    position 81, **84, 86, 87**

practice courses **80, 86,** 87, **88**
principles 90
problems 91-93
round the ring 99, 101, 102
starting off 79-83
up and down hill 90
without reins **89**
Junior Riding Test Front endpaper

Kicking 117
Kicks 161
Kimblewick 178, **179**
Knot, quick release 36, **142,** 143

Lameness 160
Laminitis 164
Laziness 113
Lead rope **39, 175**
Leading in hand 38, **39,** 141
Legs, use of the 24, 45, 55
Lice 166
Linseed 131
Loading and unloading 142-3
Lockjaw 162

Maize 131
Mane, care of the 145, 148
Markings 157
Martingales 184, **185**
Measurement of ponies 154-5
Medicine chest 167
Milk powder 134
Molasses 131, 134
Mounting 20, **21,** 117

Nappiness 114, **115**
Neckstrap **32,**79, 184
Noseband, cavesson 177, 191
   dropped 55, 98, **177,** 191
Numnahs 180, **188**
Nursing a sick pony 167

Oats 131, 134, 137, 140
Oiling leather 196
Open rein 26, **27,** 58, **104**
Overreach 153, 170

Paces, the pony's 62-64
Paddocks
   care of 124
   choice of 122-124
   feed in 124
   fences 123
   shelter 124
   size 124
   water supply in 122
Parents, notes for 11-16
Pelham, half moon 98, 178, **179**
   jointed 178, **179**

Position
   in the saddle **22, 23,** 45, **46**
   at canter 31, **32,** 53
   at trot 28, **29, 51**
   at walk 26
   of hands and arms 24, 47, **48, 51**
   of legs **22,** 24, 45, **46**
   of upper body **23,** 45, **46**
Pricked foot 154, 170
Pulling 113
Punishment 114, 118
Pony Club
   going to 72
   how to behave at 76
   objects of 7

Raincoat 186
Rearing 115
Reins, types of 180
   how to hold **24, 25, 47, 48**
   jumping without **89**
   securing 192
   taking up **25**
Rhythm 62
Riding, in forests 71
   on beaches 71
   on farmland 68
   on reserves 71
   on the road 32, 65-**68**
   over bridges, 33, 69
   up and down hill 69, **70**
Ringworm 167
Road safety 32, 65-**68**
Rope burns 172

Saddle
   carrying **187**
   cleaning 195
   general purpose 180
   good and bad **181**
   fitting 189
   parts of **181**
   putting on 186-189
   taking off 192
   tree 116, 193
Saddlery, care and cleaning 193-196
Salt 131
Salute, dressage 104
School
   exercises 74-76
   terms used in 73
   working in 74, 103-105
Seat
   general purpose 45, **46,** 84
   improving 49-52
   jumping 85
Shoeing 150-4
Shows and sports meetings 94
   classes at 97, 98

preparation for 94
Show jumping
  F.E.I. 99-101
  Horse Trials 110
  preparation for 99-100
  round the ring 99, 101-102
Shying 67, **68**
Snaffle bits, types of 178-**179**
Sprains 170
Spurs 55, 106
Staggers 165
Stirrup
  irons **182**
  altering **54**
  leathers 183, 197
  length **23, 46,** 52, 84
  length for jumping 84
Stone in foot 160
Sunburn 171
Surcingles 184
Swimming your pony 71

Tail, care of the 145
Teeth, 163
Test Sheets 19, 42-44
Tetanus 162
Tethering 143
Thin ponies 113, **135**, 162
Ticks 166
Town sections 11, 125-126
Traffic shyness 117
Transitions 26, 28, 29, 31, 56, 57, 58,
  61, 86, 103, 106
Trot
  exercises at 49
  position at 28, **29, 51**
  rising 28, **51**, 83
  sitting 28, 51, 103
  standing 52
  without stirrups 49, **50**, 51

Turning out 36
Turnout 72, 95, 97
Turns, aids for 26, **27,** 58, **104**
Tying up 36, **37,** 69, 141, **142,** 143,
  191

Unsaddling 192

Vaulting on 96
Voice, use of, 26, 27, 55, 106, 113,
  118

Walk
  on a long rein 63, **64,** 113
  position at 26, **64**
Walking a course 100, 109
Washing 149
Watering 128
Wheat 130
Whip
  changing from hand to hand 48,
  49
  dressage 186
  how to hold **48**
  type to use **183,** 186
  use of 55, **115, 118**
  use of, on circles **60**
White line 150, **151**
Windbreaks 124
Windgalls 172
Wither pad 189
Work 108, 137
Working in 96, 101, 105, 106, 109,
  110
Working paces 106
Worms 113, 163
Wounds 161-162

Young ponies 12, 119, 134, **135**